ENDURING TREASURES

ENDURING TREASURES

National Parks of the World

NATIONAL
GEOGRAPHIC
WASHINGTON, D.C.

Wrangell-St. Elias
N.P. and Preserve
UNITED STATES

Auyuittuq
National
Park Reserve
CANADA

Schiermonnikoog N.P.
NETHERLANDS

Saguenay-
St.Lawrence
Marine Park
CANADA

Mercantour N.P.
FRANCE

Yellowstone N.P.
UNITED STATES

Death Valley N.P.
UNITED STATES

Doñana N.P.
SPAIN

Barrancas del Cobre
Natural Park
MEXICO

Everglades N.P.
UNITED STATES

Tikal N.P.
GUATEMALA

Niokolo-Koba N.P.
SENEGAL

Santa Rosa N.P.
COSTA RICA

Canaima N.P.
VENEZUELA

Galápagos N.P.
ECUADOR

Manu N.P.
PERU

Torres del Paine N.P.
CHILE

Glaciers N.P.
ARGENTINA

Contents

Sareks N.P.
SWEDEN

Białowieża N.P.
POLAND

Pindos and Víkos-Aóös
Nat. Parks
GREECE

Petra N.P.
JORDAN

Tassili-n-Ajjer N.P.
ALGERIA

Nanda Devi N.P.
INDIA

Lushan N.P.
CHINA

Virachey N.P.
CAMBODIA

Tubbataha Reefs
Marine N.P.
PHILIPPINES

Nouabalé-Ndoki
N.P.
CONGO

Masai Mara Reserve
KENYA

Serengeti N.P.
TANZANIA

Mt. Kilimanjaro N.P.
TANZANIA

Komodo N.P.
INDONESIA

Kakadu N.P.
AUSTRALIA

Nitmiluk N.P.
AUSTRALIA

Great Barrier Reef
Marine Park
AUSTRALIA

Mana Pools N.P.
ZIMBABWE

Kruger N.P.
SOUTH AFRICA

Uluru N.P.
AUSTRALIA

■ Featured continental
park

■ Other park in book

Miles   3000

Kilometers   4000

Southwest N.P.
AUSTRALIA

Mt. Cook N.P.
NEW ZEALAND

Fiordland N.P.
NEW ZEALAND

*Page 1: A water lily opens its petals to
brilliant sunlight in Australia's Kakadu
National Park, which sprawls across a huge
area of the Northern Territory.*

*Pages 2-3: Photographed under a crescent
moon, Ayers Rock, a sacred Aboriginal site,
looms as the most imposing physical
feature in Australia's Uluru National Park.*

Library of Congress CIP Data appears on page 200

Introduction

Paul C. Pritchard

I'm not sure when my first "awesome" experience occurred in a park. In my childhood, awe came in small packages. Finding my first snakeskin in the local park by our house may have been it. The snake seemed awesome—as long as I was tall. My older brother and sister told me that it was from a giant poisonous python that lived in the park. I think I wanted to believe that as much as they did, but even then I knew that pythons were unheard of in West Virginia.

Parks have been the mortar in my life, bringing together my childhood, my career, my travels, my family experiences, my very self-image. Today, after decades with the National Park Service and then as the founder and head of the National Park Trust, I look back at having helped double America's national park system, at having advised the Haida peoples of Canada on how to save their home islands as parks, and at having counseled numerous nations and park advocacy groups from Ireland to China. National Park Service employees talk of being paid in sunsets. My annuity will be in having saved sunsets.

Years ago a foreign ambassador called national parks "America's greatest invention." Yellowstone, established in 1872, was the world's first national park. While there had been protected landscapes for royalty, nobility, and

Hikers in Alaska's Wrangell-St. Elias National Park make camp among the peaks of the Chugach Mountains. With 13.2 million acres, Wrangell ranks as the country's largest park.

the social elite through the ages, ours were the first parks for all the people, born of our democratic principles. Today we have more than 375 national park units in America, but equally important, the national park concept has become one of our finest exports. Some 120 nations have adopted the national park model in some manner or fashion, and the world park movement continues to grow, paralleling the democratization of more and more nations throughout the world.

When I suggested this book to the staff at the National Geographic Society, we all realized how difficult it would be to select representative parks from all the continents. With more than a thousand different units in the world's national park systems, the challenge of finding the few superlative parks for this book was frustrating. Our goal was not to create a global catalog of national parks but to give some indication of their rich diversity—the range of landscapes they encompass, from marshes to mountains, from tundra to seashores; the cultural heritages they protect; and the amazing diversity of plant and animal life they harbor.

We also wanted to tell some of the stories behind the founding and development of these precious places of our collective biosphere. Ironically, less developed nations with low population densities often find it easier to identify and set aside natural areas "untrammeled by the footprint of man." Some of these countries, like Costa Rica, claim to have met the goal proposed by the World Conservation Union (WCU) to dedicate 10 percent of their domain to national parks—far more than the 4 percent in the United States. In older nations with high population densities, such as those in Europe, it's harder to find pristine, untrammeled areas, and private lands are often included within park boundaries. But size and ownership are less important than the intent to protect the land, and its historical and natural heritage.

Hoping to provide a global forum to ensure that heritage, the WCU holds periodic conclaves for the world park movement. At one of these gatherings, in Germany, a prominent German businessman asked me to bring together European and North American park experts to advise his government. We convened in the Bayerischer Wald National Park in Bavaria, where two particular problems were presented to us. The first was the profusion of deer that was overwhelming the park's dwindling vegetation. The superintendent told us that the animals had to be penned up each winter and fed like livestock. The deer had no other home. Ironically, they moved freely through what was then the Iron Curtain. The park was their only refuge. How many should be saved, we were asked. A hard question to answer.

But it was the exhibits of dying forests in the park's interpretation center that mesmerized us. In understated narration, a harrowing scientific explanation of the effects of acid rain on the park was presented. In the forests themselves we saw areas where the bark hung from dead trees afflicted by a sort of leprosy borne on the air from outside the park. We left feeling that acid rain was our common enemy. But it took a political event—the fall of the Berlin Wall—to slow the effects of acid rain, as nations reclaimed their traditional lands, their souls. Maybe those haunting forest scenes throughout central Europe had been a call to action.

On another occasion, I took a group of experts to visit China's national parks. The government of China had asked us to examine the impact that rising waters from the Three Gorges Dam would have on several existing and potential national parks. We were taken on the Yangtze—China's Long River—traveling through the dam construction site, then upriver, occasionally making forays by motorized or poled skiffs into side tributaries. We saw a seemingly never ending series of scenic wonders: Towering rock faces, massive streams gushing out of mountain walls, ancient towns now abandoned—all would soon be gone as part of the price to harness the river's might for the future of the nation.

That has long been the critical dilemma for a world growing in population and shrinking in resources: How to juggle the needs of humans against the preservation of the natural world and the cultural legacies of the past. Increasingly, organizations like UNESCO have turned their attention to this problem, identifying International Biosphere Reserves and World Heritage sites in countries throughout the globe. At the same time, governments are recognizing the scientific value of parklands, especially as places to find new medicines and monitor the condition of the Earth's rapidly changing climate. For quite a while now, national parks have served as the planet's "canaries in the cage"; if the parks are healthy, so then is the Earth.

But sadly, neither national park health nor status is inviolate. National parks, even in this country, can lose their designation—and the protection that goes with it. I have a favorite national park spot, a place where I like to sit and stare into the Grand Canyon and listen to a solitary canyon wren as it glides over that immense chasm. Every time I am privileged to sit there, I wonder: If the Grand Canyon had not been preserved as a national park, would that special spot on the Earth still be there for me? And will it be there for the generations still to come?

SOUTH
AND CENTRAL AMERICA

Manu National Park

Joseph R. Yogerst

Macaws woke me at the crack of dawn, squawking in the branches outside my bungalow, a happy banter that echoed all around the clearing. Within minutes I was dressed and on the trail, tagging along behind Esteban Huaman, a Machiguenga guide who knows this rambling rain forest—its muddy trails, meandering rivers, and incredibly plush valleys—better than most people know their own backyards.

Our destination was Pantiacolla Peak, a half-day's hike away and the last rise of any sort before the Peruvian Andes peter out into the interminable flatness of the Amazon Basin. After a night of thunderstorms, the forest was consumed by a deep mulchy aroma that seemed to intensify with the escalating heat and humidity. Occasionally, I'd get a whiff of something much more distinct: the pungent scent of the wild garlic tree or the sweetness of a brilliant orchid. And with the incessant drone of a million cicadas punctuated by bird cries, there was never silence.

Deftly wielding his machete, Esteban whittled a bamboo shaft into a six-inch arrowhead. "This is what I used when I hunted for a living—monkey, deer, tapir, birds. But to tell you the truth," he laughed, "I was never a very good shot. I'm much better at guiding and tracking." As he would soon prove.

Farther up the trail was fresh scat, a twisted clump of bone chips and dense gray hair. "A jaguar or puma—that recently ate a sloth," Esteban said confidently. His eyes lit up as he looked around at me. "You think he lives nearby?" More evidence made it seem so: the remains of a tapir, its flesh stripped from the bones, and maggots scouring the inside of the skull. "You see the way it's scattered along the trail," said Esteban. "The tapir was attacked and pulled apart by a big cat."

Early morning mist rises above the Madre de Dios River on the eastern edge of Manu National Park. The meandering river has long been a pathway for those in quest of Manu's treasures, including the Inca, Spanish explorers, rubber barons, and modern-day tourists.

Preceding pages: Scarlet macaws feast at a clay lick along the upper reaches of the Manu River. The colorful, chatty birds use mineral salts in the clay to supplement their diet and neutralize the toxins in certain forest foods.

The kill wasn't fresh enough to set off any alarm bells. But not far away, beneath a gnarl of exposed roots, we found an animal den—just the sort of place where jaguars take refuge during big storms. Given the heavy showers of the previous evening, there was little doubt in Esteban's mind that one of the rain forest's most ferocious hunters was lurking somewhere in our vicinity.

That realization was enough to send a shiver up my spine, but it didn't faze my guide. "They rarely attack people," he said casually. And before I could ask him to clarify ("How often is rarely?"), we were off along the trail again. Creeping this time, rather than rushing, we were alert for any motion or sound. Esteban raised a hand, put a finger to his lips as a warning to be silent. An animal was nearby, something with a musky aroma. As we stooped to examine its tracks, a large beast shot across our field of vision—not the gold-and-black livery of a jaguar, but a rust colored creature, a great big collared peccary, squealing in terror as it fled into a thicket. Esteban and I exchanged nervous smiles, relieved that it was nothing more than a frightened pig.

Three hours later, we reached the summit of Pantiacolla. It was the sort of view that inspires profound silence. Nature's finest tapestry—millions of trees and the mist-covered Amazon Basin—stretched as far as the eye could see. Not a single man-made object spoiled the lush perfection. All of it, every single leaf and blade of grass, was protected within the confines of Manu National Park.

A wedge-shaped slice of the Peruvian rain forest, Manu lies just north of Cuzco. One of the world's largest tropical rain forest reserves (7,260 square miles or 4.65 million square acres), this park is in many respects the most precious relic in the entire Amazon Basin. While other parts of the rain forest have been ravaged by logging, gold mining, and oil extraction, Manu has managed to sneak into the 21st century in almost pristine condition.

Geography is the main reason why the region has remained so wild. Formidable obstacles surround the park on all three sides. Downriver are the treacherous rapids of the Rio Madeira. Upstream the mighty Andes shoot almost straight up from the forest floor to more than 13,000 feet. Protecting the area's north flank is the Fitzcarrald Isthmus, a crescent of impenetrable jungle without navigable rivers.

"Manu provides an opportunity to see how things really work in nature," says American zoologist Mercedes Foster, who has studied the park's wildlife for nearly a quarter century. "Not how things work after you've cut down half the trees, shot out all the predators, and overfished the rivers. To study a rain forest, you've got to have the integrity of all the different parts of the ecosystem, and with Manu you definitely get that."

No other park on the planet can rival Manu's incredible biodiversity. The isolated sanctuary harbors perhaps a million insect species, 15,000 different types of plants, and more than a thousand bird species (11 percent of the global total). Large neotropical mammals also thrive within its boundaries, including jaguars, tapirs, spectacled bears, giant otters, and 13 different types of monkeys. Manu is also a refuge for the Amazon's indigenous humans. Several Indian tribes call the park home, including ancient cultivators like the Piro and Machiguenga and two different groups of Stone Age nomads—the mysterious Mashco Piro and the fierce

Embracing more than 7,200 square miles and over a million species of flora and fauna, Manu (map) reigns as one of the world's most important tropical rain forest reserves.

Following pages: Laden with silt from the Andes, the Rio Pinquen snakes its way through one of the park's more secluded sections. Manu's watershed remains among the few in the Amazon Basin largely untouched by mineral or timber extraction.

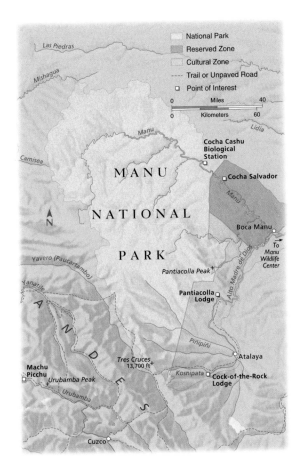

Yaminahua. The name Manu is thought to be linked to a tribe called the Manosuyo, who roamed the region during Inca times.

Since 1973, Manu has enjoyed park status. That and the arrival of tourism have smoothed some of Manu's rough edges, but this is still savage country. As recently as the 1980s, tribal war erupted when the Yaminahua began taking women and food from Machiguenga settlements along the upper reaches of the Manu River. Around the same time, a helicopter transporting Peru's president on a park tour was greeted by a fusillade of native arrows. To this day, the Mashco Piro are so elusive, so wary of outsiders, that no one has ever been able to calculate their exact number. And the vast majority of the estimated 2,000 Indians who live inside the park still make their living from primitive hunting and gathering.

There wasn't a cost-effective means to harvest Manu's abundant natural resources until the 1970s, and by then it was too late for the timber cutters and oil

On the hunt for tasty mollusks, a snail-eating snake slithers through vine blossoms in the steamy lowland rain forest. Protected by rugged mountains and fast-flowing rivers, the rain forest here remains in nearly pristine condition, supporting a vast array of plants and wildlife.

companies to exploit the land; the area already had been designated a national park.

Manu's modern guardian angel is INRENA, the equivalent of the Peruvian national park service. Keeping an iron grip on everything within the reserve, it has decreed two-thirds of the park off-limits to outsiders, including tourists, thus helping to control illegal hunting, mining, and logging, as well as proselytizing by missionaries. Scientific research is allowed within this zone, but only with official permission and under strict guidelines set by INRENA.

The remaining third of the park is divided between a reserved zone, set aside for ecotourism, and a cultural zone, where limited settlement and agriculture are currently allowed. But even in this area all visitors must use the services of an outfitter or guide licensed by the park service.

Only about 3,000 people reach Manu per year, but INRENA isn't intent on allowing more visitors. "I don't see our policies changing," head ranger Ely Velasquez told me. "There are advantages to having three zones, to keeping a large part of the park as an intangible area for research and the native communities."

Despite INRENA's vigilance, Manu isn't completely immune to the problems that have plagued other parts of the Amazon. Large international paper and pulp companies covet Manu's timber resources. Mercury levels are rising in Manu fish, most likely from gold-mining operations at Boca Colorado, upstream from the park. The pollution could affect such already endangered animals as the black caiman and giant otter; both rely on fish for the bulk of their diet.

Another threat comes from oil companies, already pumping natural gas from wells in the rain forest directly northwest of Manu. They've also undertaken seismic tests and test drilling inside the park. So far no commercially viable reserves have been discovered, but Peruvian law doesn't bar extraction from Manu if petroleum or natural gas is found in the future.

Boca Manu, a township on the park's eastern fringe, was a major hub for narcotics trafficking during the mid-1990s, and there are persistent rumors that drug smugglers still use secret airstrips inside the park to transport cocaine between Bolivia and Colombia. "We often hear planes flying low over the jungle at night," one local resident told me. "Who would be out here at such an hour except *narcotraficantes?*" Others feel that the biggest threat to Manu comes from within: a native population beginning to agitate for more political and social rights.

"I think Manu will be a totally different place 50 years from now, unless they do something about the internal population," says John Terborgh, an American scientist in charge of overseeing the Cocha Cashu biological station at Manu. "It's growing at a rate that doubles every 20 years. They're [the indigenous peoples] not allowed to exploit natural resources . . . not allowed to have firearms, chain saws, or outboard motors. So in many ways they are second-class citizens, and they're

The crown of a ceiba (kapok) tree offers a rare bird's-eye view of the surrounding forest. Soaring hundreds of feet into the canopy, ceibas are considered sacred by the Amazon's Machiguenga people, who bury their dead near the trees for safekeeping in the afterlife.

Following pages: Blue-headed and Barrand's parrots are among half a dozen avian species that gather at Manu's clay licks each morning to gorge on the mineral salts.

starting to wake up to that fact and beginning to create their own political lobby to make changes." Terborgh fears change will disturb the delicate balance of nature that makes Manu such a unique natural resource.

But for the time being that balance persists among all the special interests and opposing forces that claim a piece of Manu. It remains one of the few places in the region where the term "virgin rain forest" is not a misnomer.

The easy way to reach the park is a 45-minute flight from Cuzco to a grassy airstrip on the region's eastern fringe. But I wanted *Continued on p. 26*

Rain forest plants like passionflowers (above and below) have developed specialized pollination techniques—such as bright colors—over millions of years of evolution to attract specific insects, birds, or mammals. Most of Manu's rivers are born as streams in the cloud forest (opposite) that covers the foothills on the park's western edge.

to take an ancient trail up and over the Andes, then head into the rain forest via the Alto Madre de Dios River—a route traveled by Inca traders, Spanish explorers, and 19th-century rubber barons.

Daniel Blanco, a Peruvian ornithologist and head of a rain forest conservation group called Selva Sur, agreed to guide me as far as Atalaya, a village on the river—a journey of about 120 miles. From Cuzco, we set out in his sturdy pickup truck, making our way into the Andes along roads that clung precariously to the mountainsides. We passed ruddy-faced children, women in bowler hats, llamas traipsing across potato fields, and stone-walled houses that looked as old as Machu Picchu. And whenever I could summon the courage to look over the edge, I was sure to spot a white-water river plunging through a canyon thousands of feet below.

Above 11,000 feet, the farmland faded into windswept Andes tundra, called puna, which blankets the southern extreme of the national park. Strewn with boulders and grassy tussocks, this is the realm of the Andean condor and a wild relative of the guinea pig called the cavy. There is evidence (stone burial towers) that a pre-Inca civilization called the Lupaca once inhabited this lonely region. But otherwise the puna supports very little in the way of human life.

We pressed on toward Tres Cruces, a rocky pinnacle that marks the park's highest point (13,700 feet). The ancient Inca used to clamber up the peak to watch the summer and winter solstices. But by the time we reached the ranger station at Acjanaco, visibility had dropped to less than 20 yards; fog was so thick you could practically wrap your arms around it. Bundled inside an alpaca blanket, a young ranger shot us a cursory glance as we scaled a nearby hill. "On a clear day the view is magnificent," Daniel assured me. "You can see all the way down to the Amazon."

Given the wicked weather, we didn't linger in the highlands. As we plunged down a series of switchbacks into the Kosnipata Valley, the puna gave way to cloud forest, an incredibly quick transition from almost barren terrain to one of the globe's richest habitats. Nourished by almost constant moisture—a steady stream of clouds generated over the Amazon Basin and driven west by the equatorial trade winds—the valley supports an incredible array of flora and fauna. More than half the plants and many of the animal species are endemic, found nowhere else on Earth. "We're discovering new species all the time," Daniel related as he edged the truck around a hairpin curve. "New kinds of frogs, orchids, butterflies, and mosquitoes. The variety of life here is truly astounding."

By sundown we had checked into Cock-of-the-Rock Lodge, a small hotel nestled in the bottom of the valley. We ate dinner by candlelight (the lodge has no

Following a tradition that harkens back to the Stone Ages, a Piro Indian fishes with bow and arrow in a river that winds through the lowland forest. The Piro remain one of a half dozen indigenous tribes that inhabit the region.

Following pages: Cochas *(oxbow lakes) are a vital link in Manu's food chain; rich in aquatic life, they attract such fish-eating animals as black caimans and giant otters.*

electricity) and plotted several days of nature walks to different parts of the valley. Our main goal was to spot the lodge's namesake, the whimsical cock-of-the-rock with its bright orange headdress and curious mating rituals.

Early the next morning Daniel led me to a blind overlooking a cock-of-the-rock lek (mating area) on the banks of the Kosnipata River. We watched the birds as they cavorted for the better part of an hour, fluttering, jiggling their wings, shouting catcalls, and generally strutting their stuff. Several dozen eager males tried to impress a pair of females who seemed less than enthusiastic about the whole business. "In some ways they are so much like humans," Daniel reckoned. "No matter how well they dance or how much noise they make, some males never get chosen

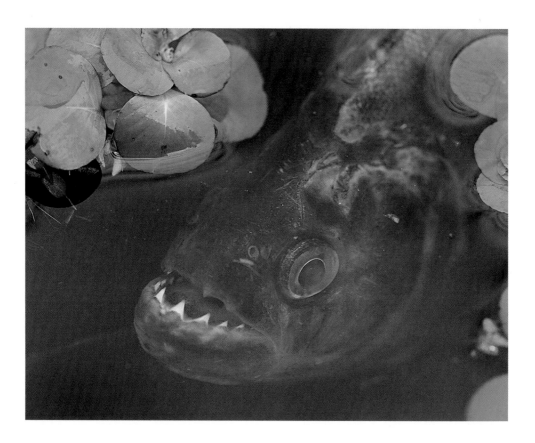

Although considered one of the more fearsome predators in the park's rivers and lakes, saw-toothed piranhas rarely attack humans.

for mating. But they come back every day and dance again. They're always hopeful."

Atalaya was another half-day's drive down the valley, a drowsy riverside town that serves as the main jumping-off point for trips on the Alto Madre de Dios and its tributaries in the eastern part of the park. This is where I hooked up with Esteban Huaman, the Machiguenga Indian who would guide me through the rest of the park. As we pulled up to the dock, he was already at work, making sure our 40-foot dugout canoe and outboard engine were set for a journey into the heart of Manu.

An extra outboard, two barrels of fuel, a battery and generator to run the radio, tents, fold-up chairs and tables, gas stove and canisters, and enough food and drinking water for several weeks in the forest were crammed into the hull, along with two crew members: Nicholas, a muscular young Piro who would pilot the boat, and Juan, an Indian from the Altiplano who would tend the kitchen. It was a full-blown expedition but no more than the bare minimum required for exploring such an isolated and inaccessible park.

After a zigzag drive across the Andes, I was relieved to be out on the water, gliding along at a leisurely pace, watching the world float by. A dense carpet of forest rose from the water's edge, reaching to clouds that hovered around the forest peaks. Here and there, occasional caimans floated on the river, and the shore was dappled with birdlife: egrets, herons, flocks of chattering parrots, and anhingas diving for food. The Alto Madre de Dios runs through the national park's cultural zone, so here and there we came across Machiguenga fishing from tiny bamboo rafts, Indian children splashing through the shallows, and isolated wooden homesteads surrounded by coca bushes and banana trees. But otherwise the river seemed little changed from what it must have been 500 years ago, when the Inca and Spanish first came this way.

The Inca called it the Amarumayu—River of the Great Serpent—after the giant anacondas living along its shores. They vigorously traded with the local tribes for jaguar skins, bird feathers, turtle oil, and coca leaves to provide a stimulant used by Inca nobles and royals. The Spanish vanquished the Inca, then tried to subdue the Manu tribes. But the local Indians—and the rugged terrain—prevailed. For the next 300 years, Manu was ignored by outsiders. It might have stayed lost and forgotten for another century if the 19th-century rubber rush had never transpired. The boom ignited a flurry of activity throughout the Amazon, as men scrambled for the "liquid gold" that oozed from rubber trees.

Carlos Fitzcarrald, a Peruvian explorer and entrepreneur, discovered a bonanza of rubber along Manu's rivers. His challenge was getting it out. In 1896, he employed 200 rubber workers to carve an eight-mile path across a forest ridge on Manu's north flank. Then he forced a thousand Indian slaves to drag a two-ton steamship up and over the ridge, a titanic—and ultimately fruitless—struggle between man and nature immortalized in the 1982 film *Fitzcarraldo* by German director Werner Herzog.

These days a much different sort of eccentric is attracted to Manu; people come in search of less tangible treasures, like solitude and silence. Raul Alfonso is one, a 59-year-old Argentine who manages Pantiacolla Lodge on the banks of the Alto Madre de Dios. I never asked his full story and he never volunteered, but something—politics, romance, or perhaps just curiosity—prompted him to flee Buenos Aires 30 years ago for a life of exile. He eventually drifted into the Amazon, where he found the peace of mind that had eluded him in more civilized environs. "People ask me what it's like living in the jungle by myself," Raul told me over breakfast one day. "There is no one out here,

Placing curiosity over safety, a squirrel monkey peers out from its rain forest perch. One of Manu's claims to fame is an unusually high variety of primates: 13 species in all, including such rare creatures as the pygmy marmoset and Goeldi's monkey.

there is nothing to do, they tell me. But here in Manu you have nothing and every-thing all at once. How can you ever get bored with this beauty all around? The ani-mals, the birds, the plants...."

Raul's closest neighbors live about 30 minutes downstream at Shipetiari, one of three Machiguenga settlements inside the park. Until the 1960s, the Machiguenga were nomads, roaming among semipermanent camps scattered throughout the region. Even now they cherish their independence and privacy. Unlike a more traditional village of tightly packed houses, Shipetiari comprises widely dispersed dwellings connected by forest trails. "This is a very typical settle-ment," said village headman David Ríos. "We have always lived spread out like this, rather than close together. My father and grandfather and great grandfather, this is how they lived. We have not forgotten."

With a rich folklore and a tradition of wandering storytellers, the Machiguenga are considered one of the area's more spiritual tribes. The residents of Shipetiari still bury their dead at the base of a giant ceiba tree, believing the tree spirit will look after their souls in the afterlife. And they still use a hallucinogenic plant called *ayahuasca*. Mashed and boiled into a tea by the village shaman, the drug is consid-ered a medium for extrasensory communication with the living and the dead.

A long day's journey downstream from Shipetiari, the Alto Madre de Dios and the Manu form a single river. But they resist the union for several miles, the muddy waters of the Manu sticking close to the left bank, the blue Madre never straying far from the right. They finally come together at a place called Boca Manu, a rowdy frontier town that serves as the main supply base and gateway for the national park. As we pulled into shore, Latino music thumped from several cantinas perched along the waterfront. Este-ban and I scrambled up a steep bank and down the town's single street, on the lookout for Leo Quinones, a Peruvian biologist who would join us for the jour-ney up the Manu into the park's inner sanctum.

We found Leo slumped in one of the cantinas, nursing a bottle of mineral water. He had bad news: The park service was dragging its feet on the permits. With a big holiday weekend coming up, it would be at least four days before we could venture any farther into the park. Rather than linger at Boca Manu, Leo suggested we spend a couple of days exploring a large private reserve called the Manu Wildlife Center, which protects a huge swath of rain forest adjacent to the park.

The wildlife center was the only place in Manu where I encountered a large number of tourists, including a group of British birders (or "twitchers," as they call themselves). "Manu is a real mecca for bird-watchers," Leo told me. "Here you have

Trekking through the needle-like anthers of a Hirtella triandra *shrub, a heteroptera bug becomes an unwitting partner in the pollination process.*

a chance to spot more species in a couple of hours than you're likely to see over an entire year in North America or Europe."

You don't have to be a twitcher to fall under the spell of Manu's birdlife, as I discovered the following morning at Blanquillo, a clay lick on the riverbank where hundreds of parrots gather each day to feast on mineral salts stored in the riverside bluff. Concealed in a floating hide anchored in the middle of the river, I watched the flocks arrive just after dawn—swarms of blue-headed and orange-cheeked parrots, and more than a hundred red-and-green macaws, clinging to vines and roots, gathering in the trees for noisy chats, then soaring away in one great mass of feathery color. It was as impressive as anything I'd ever seen in nature.

On the way back from Blanquillo, Leo and I decided to search for giant otters along a small tributary. What we found instead were Arturo and Victor, both 20-year-old woodcutters who had wandered into the forest eight days before and gotten miserably lost. Dressed in ragged T-shirts and torn jeans, they looked tired and scared as we fetched them from a muddy beach. "The mosquitoes ate us alive!"

exclaimed Victor as he crawled into the boat. For more than a week they had lived off wild berries and a few bananas, sleeping on the jungle floor at night and following the tributary by daylight, hoping it would eventually lead them out of the wilderness. It astounded me that two local kids, who ostensibly knew the forest, could get so lost in such a short time. More than anything else I would encounter in two weeks at Manu, coming across Arturo and Victor exposed how utterly wild this region remains.

The following day our permits from the park service came through—an inch-thick wad of government red tape. We were soon back on the water again, making our way up the Manu, a seven-hour trip into the heart of the park. The river along this stretch is a textbook example of fluvial dynamics, meandering back and forth in wide arcs, perpetually seeking the path of least resistance, carving new channels and creating oxbow lakes, called *cochas*, the mainsprings of life in the Amazon.

In the fast-fading light of an equatorial dusk, we pitched camp on a finger of land between the river and Cocha Salvador, our tents arrayed beneath the rain forest canopy, our kitchen perched on a bluff overlooking the water. We were a hundred miles from anything resembling civilization, but we were not alone. Far from it. Leo pointed his flashlight into the darkness. Bright red caiman eyes glared back from the spot where we had bathed just an hour before sunset.

We lingered four days at Cocha Salvador and another couple at Cocha Cashu, exploring the rain forest on foot and the lakes by canoe, and not an hour went by when there wasn't something that surprised, astonished, or even frightened me about Manu. Neon yellow butterflies swooped down to drink the tears of sideneck turtles; giant otters frolicked in the lake each morning, roughhousing with each other and trawling for piranhas; a big black caiman tried to eat one of our cooking pots, mistaking its metallic gleam for the silver flash of fish gills. And snakes of various shapes and sizes: I found an exquisite orange serpent slithering outside my tent one night—a seven foot fer-de-lance, one of the world's most venomous snakes that decided to take a shortcut through our dining area.

Manu was coming into its own, living up to its untamed reputation, an Eden that seems to get wilder by the day. But it saved the best for last. As we floated back down the river on the last morning, the clouds cleared for an instant to reveal a jagged edge of stone, the sun glistening off snowcapped peaks on the western horizon. It was a sweeping canvas from Amazon to Andes, and all of Manu was unmasked in a single glance. Like a big jungle cat, it was there one moment and then gone.

Although few in number and difficult to observe in the lush cloud forest, the Andean cock of the rock has become an abiding symbol of Manu National Park.

With annual rainfall that frequently exceeds 20 feet, Manu's high-altitude cloud forest offers more biodiversity than other parts of the park. Half the plants and a good percentage of the insects here are found nowhere else on Earth.

Other National Parks of Note

Canaima National Park

Galápagos National Park

Glaciers National Park

Canaima National Park, Venezuela

Canaima National Park presents visitors with a high-elevation challenge of a much different sort—more than a hundred forest-shrouded *tepuis* (table mountains) that form the upper reaches of Venezuela's Orinoco Basin. Much of the park's flora and fauna on the tepuis is endemic, found nowhere else on Earth. The secluded mesas soar more than 5,000 feet above the surrounding forest, and one of them serves as the backdrop for 3,212-foot Angel Falls, the world's highest cascade. Canaima is said to be the inspiration for Sir Arthur Conan Doyle's *Lost World* and Stephen Spielberg's *Jurassic Park*.

Galápagos National Park, Ecuador

Some six hundred miles off the Ecuadorian coast Galápagos National Park rises out of the ocean. It is part of an arid archipelago that harbors some of the strangest creatures on the planet, including giant tortoises that routinely live more than a hundred years, absurdly cute marine iguanas, and penguins cavorting thousands of miles away from Antarctica's ice floes. A visit to the Galápagos in 1835 provided much of the inspiration for Charles Darwin's theory of evolution.

Glaciers National Park, Argentina

Bordered by Chile's Torres del Paine National Park (see next page) on the west, spectacular Glaciers National Park ranks as Argentina's finest and most dramatic conservation area. Several large glaciers spill down from the Andes, but its most important landmark is Moreno Glacier, a 22-mile tongue of ice and snow that tumbles into the aquamarine waters of Lago Argentina, the country's largest freshwater lake. The granite Fitz Roy Range anchors the park's northern end—a true paradise for backcountry hikers and campers.

Santa Rosa National Park | Tikal National Park | Torres del Paine National Park

Santa Rosa National Park, Costa Rica

Costa Rica boasts the region's most comprehensive national park system, occupying more than 12 percent of the entire country. The vast and diverse Santa Rosa National Park sprawls across miles of picturesque Pacific coast and stretches far inland through savanna, thorn scrub, and the largest tract of dry tropical forest left in Central America—a preserve harboring many endangered animals. Santa Rosa also bears rich historical significance: It was the scene of two momentous battles that ensured Costa Rican sovereignty.

Tikal National Park, Guatemala

Guatemala's remote Tikal National Park safeguards the world's largest collection of pre-Columbian ruins—more than 3,000 Maya structures scattered across 222 square miles of virgin rain forest. Most of the larger structures, like the soaring Pyramid of the Great Jaguar, date from the Maya

Late Classic period (A.D. 550-900). Much of Tikal remains unexcavated, a tangled web of forest and stone.

Torres del Paine National Park, Chile

Located in the southern part of the country, Torres del Paine—one of the region's oldest and most impressive parks—was founded in 1962 to protect a dramatic stretch of the lower Andes. The park's namesake is a cluster of spectacular granite peaks—the largest of which soars to 10,007 feet—that present a daunting challenge to even the most experienced of mountain climbers. The rest of the park is no less impressive: broad valleys laden with glaciers, sparkling lakes, and fast-flowing rivers—a high-elevation refuge for a wide variety of Andean animals, including condors, pumas, rheas, and guanacos.

NORTH
AMERICA

Wrangell-St. Elias National Park

Joseph R. Yogerst

"It doesn't get any better than this," said Mike Thompson of the National Park Service as we glided our kayaks onto a rocky beach in the shadow of a glacier. We had just crossed Icy Bay in near-perfect conditions—bright sunshine, blue sky, and water so calm it seemed that you barely had to lift your paddle to affect forward motion. And this along an Alaska coast renowned for turbulent storms and loathsome weather.

Since tides here can reach double-digit feet, Mike decided it was best to pitch our tents on a willow-covered moraine above the beach. At dusk we were down at the shore again, cooking macaroni and cheese over a gas stove, guzzling hot chocolate, and playing hide-and-seek with a cheeky harbor seal that evidently regarded us as the evening's entertainment. "Don't let anybody tell you that rangers don't know the best campsites," Mike smiled as we reclined on a surfside boulder.

All around was raw, impetuous nature: The 18,008-foot bulk of Mount St. Elias, the world's highest coastal peak, glistening pink in the soft evening light; a rugged finger of liquid called Tsaa Fjord, choked with icebergs and crowned by more than a dozen waterfalls; and the feathery blue facade of Guyot Glacier less than half a mile away. A remnant of the last great ice age that covered North America, Guyot is slowly but surely shrinking, growing smaller by the day. On this particular evening, we could actually see it retreating, moaning and groaning as its surface cracked, calving huge hunks of ice every few minutes.

As Mike and I watched, a massive section of Guyot—maybe a hundred yards wide and a good five or six stories high—tumbled into the bay with a deafening

Although they present a fierce facade, Wrangell's grizzlies tend to shy away from humans, keeping mainly to the backcountry, where they stalk salmon and browse for berries.

Preceding pages: Guyot Glacier looms above kayakers gliding across Tsaa Fjord on the western edge of Icy Bay. The remote inlet—bounded by glaciers, waterfalls, and sheer cliffs—anchors the southern extreme of Wrangell-St. Elias National Park and Preserve.

crash. A pressure wave rolled out from the splash zone, gray and menacing, headed straight for us. But like a couple of deer caught in headlights, Mike and I were too mesmerized to move. I thought to myself, the wave will peter out before it gets this far. But it didn't. It kept advancing, building speed and height as it pushed rapidly across the bay. "Let's go!" Mike shouted, shoving me toward the moraine, and we scrambled onto higher ground just before the wave swept over the rock where we'd been standing.

Nature is often an unforgiving host in Alaska's Wrangell-St. Elias National Park and Preserve. Nearly everyone I came across during two weeks of exploring the park had tales of survival—people stranded on mountains, washed down rivers, attacked by bears, lost in planes. And nearly every day I witnessed nature's fickle temper with my own eyes. Almost a quarter century of national park status has done little to tame rough and rugged Wrangell, which remains wild at heart.

The most imposing challenge is sheer scale. Wrangell's 13.2 million acres could easily absorb the 11 largest national parks in the lower 48. And lumped together with adjoining nature reserves—Alaska's Glacier Bay, the Yukon's Kluane, and British Columbia's Tatshenshini-Alsek Provincial Park—this is the single largest wilderness area on the planet.

Everything about the park is big and bold. Four major mountain ranges converge here, sprouting 9 of the continent's 16 highest peaks. Surrounding these summits is the world's largest accumulation of subpolar ice—more than 150 glaciers and ice fields larger than several American states. Their runoff feeds a dozen major rivers, some so ruthless during spring melt they are virtually unrunnable in any sort of craft.

"It's not only beautiful, it's so dynamic," chief of interpretation Ed Roberts told me during a visit to the park headquarters and visitor center at Copper Center. "You hike up a creek and camp and next day you've gotta cross a stream that wasn't there yesterday." Staring out the window, Ed pointed his chin at three massive peaks that dominate the park's northwest corner—Sanford, Drum, and Wrangell, all of them snowcapped and more than 12,000 feet in elevation. "It's remarkable. I don't think you can lose your awe for the place."

Another thing that sets Wrangell apart from many other national parks is human activity. Subsistence hunting, fishing, and trapping by local residents is allowed throughout the park; sport hunting is permitted in the preserve. Airplanes, snowmobiles, and all-terrain vehicles are considered legitimate access tools because without them vast sections of the park would be virtually inaccessible. Nearly a million acres of the park are still in private hands, including vast tracts owned by Alaska native corporations, who have the right to harvest timber and mine on their lands if they so desire.

"Our wilderness has a different definition," said chief ranger Hunter Sharp, also based at Copper Center. "In the lower 48 we're very accustomed to managing 'set aside' lands in which we control every aspect of what goes on in them. But that is not the pattern here in Alaska, where we are engaged in trying to fit people who are a part of the landscape into the continuation of the park. Humans have been here for millennia, and we are going to continue to be here." Diversified land use was the compromise that President Jimmy Carter was willing to strike in order to create Wrangell and half a dozen other Alaska parks through the Alaska National Interest Lands Conservation Act (ANILCA) in 1980.

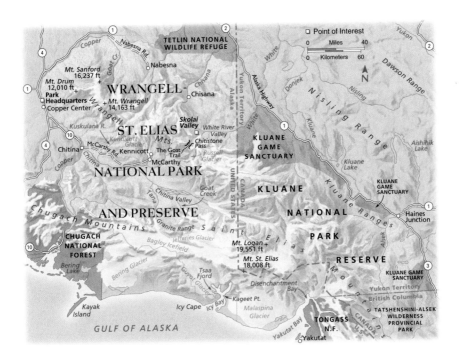

Wrangell's rugged topography extends from glacier-choked bays along the Gulf of Alaska to boreal forests in the upper reaches of the Yukon Basin.

Following pages: Flowing down from the Wrangell Mountains, swirls of ice and stone form Nizina Glacier. Drawn by the allure of quick riches, thousands of prospectors trekked this valley in 1913 on their way to the Chisana goldfields.

   National park status has given Wrangell a much higher global profile, but rugged nature and utter remoteness keep visitor numbers at fewer than 32,000 per year. The park doesn't boast a single paved road and has barely a hundred miles of gravel road. There are few marked trails and just one campground, which is pretty much how the Park Service wants things to stay. "I don't think this park really should ever have four-lane paved access," said Edmond Roberts. "It would change what Wrangell is about. This park is so massive, and there are so many natural barriers out there, I don't think you could ever put in enough roads to see some parts of it."

   My plan was to explore the park from south to north, by water and by land, by foot, car, and kayak. Starting on the lush Gulf of Alaska coast, I would work my way inland to the state's sprawling tundra zone. First stop was Yakutat, an isolated

fishing village on the Alaska Panhandle outside the park's southeast corner. As my flight from Anchorage touched down, a steady drizzle shrouded the landscape but could not hide the fact that Yakutat perches on the very edge of the wilderness. As I drove into town, a mother bear and two cubs scampered across the airport road beneath the steely gaze of a bald eagle perched high in a huge fir tree.

One of Alaska's oldest permanent settlements, Yakutat is isolated, accessible only by air or sea, and the weather is often downright dreary. "It's the most beautiful place in the world when the sun shines," boasted Keith Johnson as I checked into cozy accommodations at the Mooring Lodge. "It's a great place to live, a great sense of community here." Like many of the people I found residing in and around the park, Keith has a family tree firmly rooted in Wrangell. His father was born in Chitina, a tiny pioneer town on the park's western edge, and his grandfather worked the famous copper mines at Kennicott during the 1920s. His wife, Sue, is a native Tlingit, raised in Yakutat.

The rain had cleared by the following morning, bathing Yakutat in brilliant sunshine framed by snowy peaks. Standing front and center was pyramid-shaped St. Elias, North America's fourth highest peak after Denali, Logan and Orizaba. As I stood at the edge of Yakutat Bay, watching the fog burn off, I realized this must have been much the same view that Danish explorer Vitus Bering enjoyed when he anchored here in 1741 during his landmark journey for the Russian tsar. In Denmark it was St. Elias Day, so Bering figured that would be a good name for the awe-inspiring peak.

The task of flying Mike Thompson and me out to Icy Bay fell to veteran bush pilot Les Hartley. Piper, a frisky black labrador, was patiently waiting beside his plane. "That dog just loves to fly," Les smiled. "She'll fly all day if you let her. And she never gets airsick . . . except for that time we gave her some bad salmon." Within minutes we were soaring over Malaspina, the biggest piedmont glacier in North America—more than 50 times larger than the island of Manhattan. I had always thought of glaciers as essentially blue or white. But Malaspina bears a frozen coat of many colors—gray, black, orange, brown, and white—sinuous bands of ice, stone, and sand that mark its advance over the years. The outer edge is scarred by depressions filled with crater lakes that bring a splash of turquoise and milky jade green to the landscape.

Deep inside Kennicott Glacier, a waterfall plunges through an ice cave. Subterranean streams and caverns honeycomb the glacier's thick mass.

"Awful lot of rugged country," Les mused. "I've never landed down there and never want to. You'd probably survive, but I hate to think what would happen to the plane with all those sinkholes. Some pretty big trees grow over on the southwest side of Malaspina, and every so often a sinkhole will just swallow one of 'em up." Les touched down on the beach at Kageet Point, where Mike and I assembled our portable kayaks with two companions: National Park Service photographer Joshua Foreman and Student Conservation Association volunteer Neil Davy from Oxford University in England. During the next four days, we kayaked around the western extremities of Icy Bay on a routine ranger patrol. "We come here twice each summer to see what's going on," Mike explained. "Make sure there are no hunters or poachers, inventory campsites, and check the recession rates of the glaciers."

At times it was tough going, the pack ice so thick we had to gouge a path through the fjords with our paddles. Driving rain and swell broke over the bows of our kayaks. But around every turn was more of the eccentric, untamed beauty that makes Wrangell unique—600-foot waterfalls that have never been named, icebergs flecked with gravel spots, and the ghostly remnants of an evergreen forest that flourished before the last ice age.

Leaving our kayaks behind, we walked up and over a mammoth moraine called the Arrowhead that rends the face of Guyot Glacier. In the middle of the moraine is a valley with a remnant glacier that split from Guyot several years ago, and running through the middle of the remnant is a gymnasium-size ice cavern with an entrance shaped like a mosque dome. Beams of sunshine burst through gaps in the roof, casting an eerie aquamarine glow that lit our way through the frozen cave. I pressed my tongue against the wall, licking up ice-cold water that hadn't seen daylight in perhaps ten thousand years.

The blue skies had faded into a late summer squall, and the temperature had plunged from the 60s into the 40s by the time we paddled back to Kageet Point. But that didn't dampen Mike's enthusiasm for the landscape. "I've been a ranger in this part of Wrangell for three years and every day seems like the first. I still get so excited about the glaciers, the weather, the mountains. It's an awesome place. You never seem to get jaded."

As the eagle flies, the rugged McCarthy-Kennicott area in the heart of the park is only about a hundred miles from the coast. But the only way to reach it from Icy Bay (without my own wings) was by hopping a bush plane back to Yakutat, a commercial flight west to Anchorage, and driving eight hours east across south-central Alaska.

The last 60 miles is along the rough-and-tumble McCarthy Road, one of the

Nature's amazing symmetry runs riot through a glacial debris field. Sometimes buried for thousands of years in hard-packed ice, stones like these are often transported dozens of miles before they again see the light of day.

state's most scenic drives. Renowned for its deep potholes and brutal washboards, the gravel track follows the bed of the Copper River and Northwestern Railway, which once transported copper from the mine at Kennicott to the docks at Cordova. This is not a route for anyone with vertigo: The road leaps the Kuskulana River on a one-way railroad trestle that hangs 238 feet above raging white water. At the end of the road, across the Kennicott River, is the town of McCarthy, unofficial capital of the Wrangell realm and one of the quirkiest towns in outback Alaska.

Founded in 1910 as a supply center for the nearby copper mine, the town soon grew into an amusement center for off-duty miners. Drinking, gambling, and prostitution were its major industries, and even though the vices faded away after the mine shut in 1938, McCarthy has preserved its capricious ways. Think of the town in the TV series *Northern Exposure*—only with half as many people and twice as many eccentrics—and you have some idea of what makes McCarthy tick. Until a footbridge was completed in 1997, the only way to reach the town from the end of the road was by pulling yourself over the turbulent Kennicott River on a hand tram

A study in blue and white, the Bagley Icefield stretches nearly a hundred miles along the park's southern flank, one of the world's largest tracts of subpolar ice.

suspended from a cable. Telephone service is another recent phenomenon, but residents with vehicle problems must still wait until the winter freeze before they can drive their vans or trucks across the river and down to Anchorage for repairs. Yet locals seem to thrive on the wilderness experience. "Having bears walk through my front yard is one of the reasons I live here," says Betty Adams, proprietor of the McCarthy Lodge, a hotel and saloon.

McCarthy sports only about 50 year-round residents—people intrepid enough to brave winters with temperatures that routinely dip to minus 40°F. But come the big thaw, several hundred seasonal residents and summer workers flood the town, a blend of rugged individuals and New Age nature lovers, hunting guides and bush pilots, all seeking their own brand of solitude and satisfaction in the wilderness.

A couple of miles upriver from McCarthy is the old copper mine at Kennicott, dominated by the concentration mill, where the ore was crushed into smaller and smaller pieces. A giant beast of a building, it towers 14 stories above the valley floor. Registered as a national historic landmark and considered one of the nation's most endangered historic properties, Kennicott is now a ghost town. But between 1911 and 1938 it buzzed with activity, a self-contained company town with more than a thousand residents and some of Alaska's most unusual contrivances—including a baseball diamond hacked into the side of a glacier and steam-heated sidewalks so miners wouldn't have to shovel snow in winter.

I spent several hours exploring the town with Christy Swindling, a geology student from University of California-Santa Cruz who had snagged a summer job giving walking tours of historic Kennicott. "The Russians came through here on several expeditions in the 1700s, and they found native Ahtna who traded copper," she explained. But nobody actually discovered the contact zone until the summer of 1900 when a couple of veteran prospectors—Tarantula Jack Smith and Clarence Warner—arrived in the area. "They saw this green patch up on the hillside and figured it was a meadow where they could graze their horses. But that green patch was a huge outcrop of copper that had oxidized."

Their discovery was nothing short of phenomenal, 70 percent pure chalcocite copper with traces of gold and silver. Excitement swept the mining industry, and even though the site was extremely remote, tycoons such as J. P. Morgan and the Guggenheim Brothers were among those who rushed to invest in the mine. During its 27 years of operation, the mountain behind Kennicott yielded more than 200 million dollars worth of copper and silver ore. Yet the complex was abandoned almost as rapidly as it was built. "The only way out was on the last ore train," Christy related. "Residents left nearly everything behind in their mad dash to leave—dishes in sinks, completely furnished houses, half-burned logs in wooden stoves."

With the copper depleted, the region settled into a modern "ice age" during which it was largely forgotten by the outside world. Then in the 1970s a new sort of pioneer started arriving in Wrangell—not miners or trappers but young adventure enthusiasts who recognized the untapped potential of such a grand and challenging landscape. One of them was Bob Jacobs, a Utah-born, Colorado-raised mountain climber and glacier guide who has called McCarthy home for more than 20 years. A veteran of Everest and Denali expeditions, Bob agreed to guide me through some of the more spectacular parts of the Wrangell backcountry.

With his 12-year-old son Ian in tow, Bob and I hopped a bush plane down to Iceberg Lake in the upper reaches of the Tana River Basin. Wedged between two nameless glaciers and a dozen anonymous peaks, the lake was as calm as a sheet of glass. The soft glacial silt around the shore was full of tracks—Dall sheep, mountain goats, and several grizzly, among others. "A sow and two cubs by the looks of it," said Bob. Later on, we saw them on the hillside *Continued on p. 62*

With an eye out
for crevasses and
water-filled, cave-size
holes called moulins—
which could swallow
rider and cycle without
a trace—an intrepid
biker makes his way
across Root Glacier.

Following pages: Lush
coniferous forests
and intermittent
marshlands dominate
the northern third of
Wrangell-St. Elias.
A rough-and-tumble
dirt track called the
Nabesna Road is the
only land route to this
secluded wilderness.

Wrangell's rugged topography provides refuge for many of North America's largest mammals, including bears, caribou, moose, Dall sheep, and nimble mountain goats (right) that graze the park's highest slopes. Sport hunting is banned in the national park zone but permitted in the preserve area under very strict conditions: number of permits issued, season length, and bag limits.

Kennicott ghost town—a beehive of copper-mining activity during its heyday from 1911 to 1938—is now the park's most popular attraction, a national historic landmark dominated by the 14-story concentration mill (at right), where ore was reduced to pebbles.

above our camp, the mother browsing for berries, the cubs romping behind, barely able to keep pace with her massive strides.

Several days later we found ourselves trekking across a much different Wrangell landscape—the high-latitude tundra and taiga of Skolai Valley, about 30 miles northeast of McCarthy. Even the season seemed to be different in this part of the park. Though it was only late August, the foliage was already changing from its dark summer green into the bright reds and yellows of autumn, and a definite chill was in the air, the temperature hovering just above freezing as we pitched our tents in a grove of stunted willows.

Skolai is the park's number-one backcountry destination and perhaps the only place where you're likely to run into other trekkers. Sure enough, someone wandered into our camp around sundown: a gray-haired lady with a sketchbook and pencil box tucked under her arm. "This place is magic," said Barbara Moorford, who had come all the way from Madison, Wisconsin, to render Wrangell's dramatic landscape. "I'd flown over these mountains on previous trips to Alaska and finally decided that I had to explore them on foot."

The following day I followed Bob and Ian up the Goat Trail, a precipitous route that climbs more than 1,800 feet to Chitistone Pass. From 1913 until the early 1920s, the trail served as the main route for miners headed for the gold rush at Chisana in what is now the east-central sector of the park. "But it's definitely not a white man's route," Bob explained to me as we plodded our way upward. "The Ahtna once used this as their trade route from the coast into the interior. As soon as you get past here, the whole Yukon is wide open. You can hike all the way to the Arctic Ocean."

By the time we finally reached Chitistone, the drizzle had faded into light snow. But even in this desolate landscape there was no shortage of wildlife; a herd of Dall sheep poised on one flank of the pass and dainty purple forget-me-nots (the Alaska state flower) scattered across the windswept tundra. Hunched behind a boulder, we quickly ate our lunch. When the sun crept out, we ambled over to the edge of the pass, gazing down into a great wilderness of stone, ice, and water. To the north, beyond Russell Glacier, we could see the White River Valley, one of the wildest and least known parts of Wrangell, and a literary landmark of sorts. A key scene of Jack London's *Call of the Wild* takes place along the banks of the White River—the part where the canine hero, Buck, first encounters John Thornton, the man who will set him free.

My own liberation in the wilderness came with Paul Claus, a veteran Wrangell bush pilot who dares to go places and do things that few aviators would even imagine. Paul's father, John, staked claim to five acres at the isolated eastern end of the Chitina Valley in the early 1960s, a riverside plot that eventually grew into a wilderness guiding business and a rustic lodge. The Claus spread is dubbed "Ultima Thule" after the ancient Greek term for Europe's northern extremes, at the outer edge of the civilized world.

Nowadays the lodge has enough creature comforts to attract a steady stream of Hollywood stars and Wall Street types who like their wilderness with hot showers and central heating. But otherwise the name is apt. If you don't count the gray wolves and grizzly bears that inhabit the nearby woods, the nearest neighbors are 20 miles away.

The only way to reach Ultima Thule is by flying, which just happens to be

The park draws its name from two adjacent mountain ranges (opposite): the volcanic Wrangell Mountains (foreground) and the granitic St. Elias Mountains in the distance. Together they harbor nine of the continent's sixteen highest peaks. Summer brings a blaze of floral glory to the high country, where saxifrage bloom on the tundra (above).

Paul's abiding passion. He earned his solo license at 14 and bought his first air-craft a couple of years later, at about the same age that other kids learn to drive. "He has a gift," says a friend who lives in McCarthy, "a natural ability in the air." I confess that I'm normally a nervous flier, especially in small planes. But with Paul at the controls of his Super Cub or vintage Beaver—working the machines like extensions of his physical being—I settled into an amazing calm the minute we lifted off the ground. And a good thing, too, because flying is the only way to explore vast stretches of Wrangell-St. Elias that are normally beyond the pale of human experience. "Ninety-nine percent of this park is inaccessible by road," Paul explained. "But with an aircraft you can touch down just about anyplace." Soon enough I would discover that he wasn't kidding.

"Hey, you want to land in some cool places?" Paul asked that first morning at Ultima Thule. We climbed into the Super Cub with his wife, Donna, and winged our way up the Chitina Valley and into a menacing gnarl of ice and stone called the Granite Range. Far below, a huge grizzly ambled across a sandbar in the middle of a river, probably on the lookout for salmon. And on a windswept hillside we spot-ted a female black bear and her cubs browsing for berries. "How 'bout we land up there?" smiled Paul, pointing at a precipitous cliff above Goat Creek. I felt my heart skip a beat. But Paul executed a perfect landing on a strip of tundra no more than a hundred yards long.

We hopped out and moved toward the edge of the cliff. Through binoculars we could see Dall sheep grazing steep slopes on the opposite side of the valley. But that wasn't close enough for Paul. Moments later we were back in the Super Cub, zipping along the edge of the cliff, almost within touching distance of those same animals. "Look at that boy down there!" Paul enthused about a cluster of sheep with full-curl horns. "You don't see 'em that big very often. You're looking at near world-record rams."

Farther up the valley, Paul guided the plane into a tight corkscrew dive. I fig-ured we were going in for a closer look at the glacier below. But seconds later we were sitting on the glacier after another seemingly impossible touchdown between parallel crevasses. "Wow!" was all I could manage to say as I caught my breath. Stand-ing on the ice, squinting into the glare of the sun, Paul very modestly explained how he got to be so good at landing in tricky spots. "I've spent so much time walking and skiing the same terrain. That way you get to know the different types of ice and snow, what the surface conditions are really like. I once skied the entire Bagley Ice-field—400 plus miles in 40 days—camping on the snow and ice every night. How many pilots can say that?"

Taking off from the glacier, Paul pulled back on the throttle and we soared high into the heavens once again. All of Wrangell spread out before us, a panorama

With more than 90 percent of the park inaccessible by road, bush planes offer the only realistic means of exploring the Wrangell backcountry.

Following pages: Bathed in the pink glow of twilight, 14,163-foot Mount Wrangell seems to hover above the Copper River Valley. The park's only active volcano, Wrangell last erupted in 1900 but often exhales steam plumes visible far and wide on clear, cold days.

that took in several hundred miles of wilderness in every direction—snowy peaks and volcanoes, countless glaciers, and vast river valleys—the very essence of Alaska's wild heart.

But we weren't the only ones taking in the view. Gliding beside us was a lone hawk, curiously gazing our way, mimicking our banks and dives, testing the mettle of this strange mechanical creature that had strayed into its realm. Paul wasn't quite as skilled as the hawk, but he was darn close. And for a brief instant, perhaps the only time in my life, I knew what it was like to fly like a bird.

Thousands of years of rain and wind have weathered the surface of Jefferies Glacier on the edge of the Bagley Icefield. Surrounded by dozens of nameless peaks and glaciers, Jefferies lies in a virtually unexplored corner of Wrangell-St. Elias, adjacent to the Canadian border.

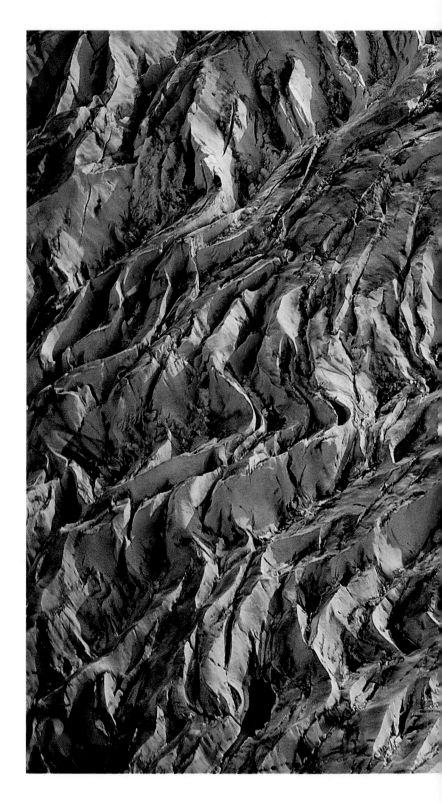

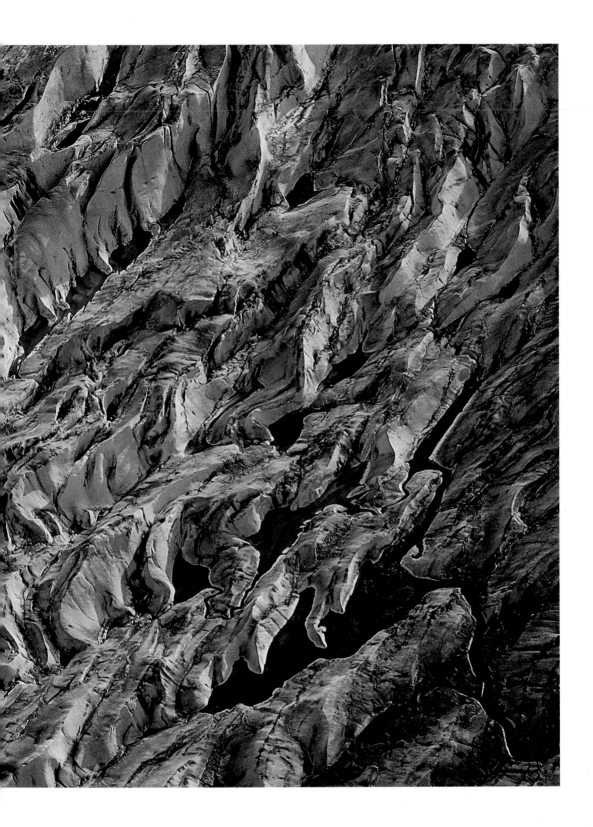

Other National Parks of Note

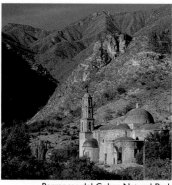

Auyuittuq National Park Reserve   Barrancas del Cobre Natural Park   Death Valley National Park

Auyuittuq National Park Reserve, Canada

A large chunk of Canada's Arctic wilderness lies on Baffin Island within Auyuittuq National Park. The name means "land that never melts" in the Inuit language, and indeed large parts of the park are buried beneath glaciers and ice fields. The stark granite peaks of the Penny Ice Cap reach more than 7,000 feet, presenting a stiff challenge for climbers. Other attractions include rugged coastal scenery and typical Arctic animals, like polar bears and caribou. Villages around the park's edge give a glimpse into the everyday life and artistic heritage of the local Inuit people.

Barrancas del Cobre (Copper Canyons) Natural Park, Mexico

The massive Barrancas del Cobre Natural Park sprawls across a large section of Chihuahua state in northern Mexico. A network of deep gorges—four of them deeper than Arizona's Grand Canyon— gives the area its name. But the terrain is also marked by rugged highlands and evergreen forests. The 50,000 Tarahumara constitute the largest of the four Indian tribes that live here, giving the region its rich cultural heritage. Although the park is crisscrossed by hiking trails, the most popular way to explore Copper Canyons is via the Chihuahua al Pacifico Railway.

Death Valley National Park, U.S.

Death Valley National Park is America's largest desert preserve, 3.4 million acres of arid wilderness astride the border between California and Nevada. Protected since 1933 as a national monument, Death Valley received full park status in 1994. Flanked by towering mountains, the valley flaunts sand dunes, volcanic craters, chromatic gorges, and the continent's lowest point (282 feet below sea level at Badwater). Despite its ominous climate and menacing terrain, the park also boasts its share of human history—relics of gold-rush days and wagon trains gone astray.

Everglades National Park   Saguenay-St. Lawrence Marine Park   Yellowstone National Park

Everglades National Park, U.S.

America's largest remaining subtropical wilderness is protected within the confines of Florida's 1.4-million-acre Everglades National Park. This vast expanse of saw grass, peppered with hardwood hammocks and cypress stands, is home to more than 300 bird species and such rare mammals as the Florida panther and the manatee. Its most famous denizen is the alligator, best seen on boat safaris or from elevated walkways built over the fragile wetlands.

Saguenay-St. Lawrence Marine Park, Canada

One of Canada's newest nature reserves, Saguenay-St. Lawrence Marine Park, in Quebec, is situated at the confluence of the Saguenay and St. Lawrence rivers. The park embraces some of Canada's most impressive coastal scenery, including the mountainous shores of Saguenay Fjord. Several whale species—minke, fin, humpback, pilot, and blue (the world's largest creature)—flock here to feed in warmer months. Even an endangered population of beluga whales is found in these cold waters.

Yellowstone National Park, U.S.

The world's first national park, Yellowstone was signed into existence by the U.S. Congress in 1872. The park's 2.2 million acres encompass part of the Rocky Mountains and much that's grand about the American West—dramatic waterfalls, deep canyons, the world's largest geyser field (including Old Faithful), and abundant wildlife (grizzly bear, bison, moose, and bald eagles). Modern-day controversies like traffic congestion, reintroduction of the timber wolf, and mining on the park periphery put Yellowstone at the forefront of national park planning and policy-making.

EUROPE

Mercantour National Park

Text by Patrick Booz
Photographs by Vincent J. Musi

Long before I saw what was coming, I could hear the tramping, clanging, and clamor, like the approach of a weird army of percussionists. Closer came the tumult until I could make out barks, whinnies, and bleats. Then suddenly, around the corner of this narrow mountain road, an ascending phalanx confronted me. At least 2,000 sheep plodded forward, their small wooden bells clinking and rattling, the flock sprinkled here and there with shaggy goats, mules, and horses. Happy dogs yipping at the edges helped keep the army moving. At front and rear marched clusters of shepherds, moving methodically, occasionally using short whips to control renegades and stragglers.

I pressed against the steep hillside, but on came the crush, flowing around me—a sea of woolly backs each painted with a number. The leaders sported pom-poms of red, blue, and orange; the goats crashed past with outsize neck bells bonging. The entire flock created a musky, lanolin-tinged cloud that wafted up the valley.

Without warning, I found myself caught up in an age-old practice known as transhumance, a word with Latin roots—*trans*, across, and *humus*, earth—the seasonal shifting of animals, sheep especially, between low valleys and Alpine pastures. This tradition has continued at least since Roman times 2,000 years ago. The annual up-and-down migration has been a fixture of Alpine existence, and it takes on an almost mythical quality, with plenty of wine and frivolity marking the successful conclusion of each stage.

This lucky encounter took place at the northern edge of Parc National du Mercantour (Mercantour National Park) in the high Alps of southeastern France.

Summer residents of Mercantour National Park in France's southern Alps, a flock of 2,000 sheep follows a seasonal grazing routine in place here for 2,000 years.

Preceding pages: From June through October, shepherd Philippe Carinier and his dog Tarzan watch over thousands of sheep in the park's Came des Fources district. Small herds of cattle also wander the park, wintering in vacheries, small barns that dot the landscape.

The park extends for 50 miles like an elongated letter *s* turned on its side, winding south and east from the Alps of Haute-Provence, along the Italian border, and through the Maritime Alps to within ten miles of the Mediterranean Sea. Close to the park's southern limit stand the Riviera resorts of Menton and Monaco and the coastal city of Nice.

The park covers 265 square miles, though its land is surrounded by a *zone périphérique* (peripheral zone) twice as large. In Europe, where national parks tend to be small in comparison to the great expanses of protected land in North America, the peripheral zone takes on special significance. Here I met villagers and townsfolk whose traditional life of forestry and herding has been thrown into flux by tourism. I found myself affronted by ski resorts with wall-to-wall shops and fast-food outlets, but also enchanted when, lost in a maze of stone alleyways, I discovered a humble chapel with wood shingles. Around its corner, I nearly bumped into a stooped woman leading her single cow to pasture. While the peripheral zone may contain roads, towns, and new developments, it still gives a taste of Western Europe's last remnant of peasant life. Also, in places where the park is only one mile wide, the zone serves as a vital buffer and helps sustain various ecosystems and species that require ample room to roam.

The name Mercantour means "limit" or "boundary." It was first the name of a 9,094-foot mountain on France's border with Italy. The name was later applied to the surrounding range, and finally to the park itself. Founded in August 1979, Mercantour became the sixth of France's seven national parks, enclosing terrain that had long been a royal hunting reserve for Italian dukes. Today, some half a million visitors come each year to enjoy the mountain wildlife and scenery and, inside the peripheral zone, to take up such sports as rock climbing, skiing, river rafting, paragliding, off-trail biking, and horseback riding. No such activities are permitted within the park boundaries, and true lovers of nature come for the mountain walking and ecological bounty of the core.

From its lowest point in deep river gorges, the park has a vertical rise of nearly two miles to its summit, the 10,312-foot-high Cime du Gélas. Such a rise, as in mountain regions worldwide, accounts for the many ecosystems and the great biological diversity. In Mercantour a hiker can walk from the baked soil of lowland olive groves to the high realm of Alpine orchids in a single day. Three factors shape the diversity of plant and animal life: the broken landscape, with its striking highs and lows and isolated valleys; the continental climate of mainland Europe in the northern half of the park; and in the south the tempering warmth of the Mediterranean.

I decided to walk the full length of the park, from Larche in the north to Sospel in the south. The five-day trek would follow a series of well-marked, well-maintained trails—part of a system throughout France known as the GR (*grande randonnée*, great walk). Here known as the GR 5, it follows the arc of the Alps southward and is among the country's most difficult because of its high-altitude traverses. It is also perhaps the most celebrated walk in France.

During my first day I marched uphill to a windy pass that would lead me down into the heart of Mercantour. I encountered the army of sheep halfway up to the Cime de la Bonette, a pass with uninhibited views of the wild mountains cascading south toward the sea. At stony elevations far above the tree line, the Alps are a

Tightly hugging the Italian border, Mercantour National Park stretches for 50 miles from the Alps of Haute-Provence to within 10 miles of the Mediterranean Sea.

Following pages: Reflected in a mountain lake, the peaks above Lac d'Allos in the park's western section begin to blend into the evening sky.

light putty gray, raw and hard. To reach the highest outcrops for the best panorama, I inched my way sideways around an abutment, only to expose myself to a blast of wind that flattened me—literally blew me down. I then crawled to a stone for protection, where I huddled, wind whipping my face, and gloried in the harsh vista.

The word alp originally meant "mountain meadowland," though now the term describes any high, snowy peak. The great crescent of the Alps, Europe's major mountain chain, arcs through seven countries, from Slovenia in the east, through Austria, Germany, Liechtenstein, Switzerland, Italy, and France. Here, at its western extent, the mountains come down to the sea. These Maritime Alps—sharp, craggy, and abrupt at a youthful five million years old—have had their faces and valleys scoured

and scraped by glaciers of the last ice age. Throughout Mercantour, rich mixtures of multihued granite and sedimentary rocks are pressed, enfolded, thrust up, and planed, revealing the geologic history of these mountains: U-shaped glacial valleys, smoothed and tilted rock faces, sapphire lakes.

From the Cime de la Bonette, a steep descent—hard on the knees and ankles—took me headlong toward the valley of the Tinée River far below. Barren rock turned to scrub, scrub turned to short grass, and soon I was walking knee-deep through meadow grass and wildflowers. Hordes of grasshoppers clung to the stems of the sun-soaked plants; the sound of their throbbing, rhythmic vibration seemed to electrify the mountainside. In a frenzy to escape my footsteps, they leapt and flew and fell to earth in clouds, becoming entangled in my shoelaces and trouser cuffs.

The meadows lay as if painted by a pointillist's brush, forcing me to stop and admire the myriad blossoms. Of France's 4,200 species of plants, nearly half grow here. Orchids especially thrive, with 64 of the country's 150 species. A remarkable 34 types of endemics—species that live here and nowhere else in the world—are found in Mercantour's remote valleys. Near a spray of purply thrift I discovered a spring that gushed straight from a rocky hollow; I drank the cold crystal water until my teeth hurt, then followed the little rill downstream. As trees started to flank the fields, pink and white wild roses gave way to brilliant splashes of yellow mountain broom dotted among the heavy greens of pines, their complex flowers drooping in great numbers like golden rain.

Ahead of me I saw on a bank of damp sand what looked like a nest of wavering leaves. Up close I found a swarmed mass of butterflies, some blue and violet, others yellow and orange, most powder green with striking black-veined wings. They all came to lap at the wetness, safe from the rushing water a few feet away. Groups of 50 or 60 of them huddled tightly together. I wet my hand in the stream and put it close to the butterflies. One climbed aboard my wrist, slowly unfurled its long black proboscis, and tickled me as it searched for liquid.

At day's end a patch of color across a ravine revealed another person, a red-bearded shepherd in checked shirt and beret, gnawing a cheroot as he ambled behind his several hundred sheep. He drove the flock toward his rustic mountain hut through soft, streaming evening light. Distant shadows mottled the mountains and sent ripples across pine-clad slopes. As the shepherd slowly disappeared into the last light, I was left in the beautiful solitude of the place.

Rules of the park state that visitors can overnight but not stay for days in the same place. During the walk I often slept in my orange one-man tent. To travel light

Sunset silhouettes the foothills along Cime de la Bonette pass. In winter, roadside posts serve as markers on snow-covered routes leading to fast-growing ski regions at higher elevations.

Following pages: At the park's western slopes, the Vallon de la Gordolasque reveals itself through rain and fog. Italian dukes used the park's countryside as their personal hunting grounds until the land was turned over to France in the 1800s.

I carried no stove, so bread, cheese, a piece of fruit, and a few mouthfuls of water became my breakfast. But a joy of long walks in this part of France comes from the chance to descend for a good meal. I would occasionally splurge by going to a hotel or simple hostel to savor hot food, a hot bath, and clean sheets.

My third day of hiking, the longest of all, was the most challenging—onto the steep, barren slopes of Mont Mounier in the park's west-central region. From studying my map, I knew I would pass just beneath the mountain's 9,242-foot peak, then walk the length of a ridge that fell precipitously to the left before I'd find a manageable trail. The morning began with broken clouds, and I could see above me the

summit rising in all its crumpled geologic detail. With sudden swiftness, however, the sky turned an ominous blue-black. Mont Mounier faded to a brooding silhouette as rain swept down, followed by snow. Within minutes I was stranded in a raging blizzard. I could discern no depth, no texture in the landscape, no horizon, and for the first time in my life I understood the expression "whiteout." A sickening feeling of vertigo enveloped me as I struggled downhill. Yet at the same time a kind of animal instinct took hold to keep me headed in the right direction.

"Lose altitude," I kept telling myself. "Lose altitude, but don't lose your life." With visibility at times hardly more than the length of my arm, I came perilously close at one point to the ridge's rim, but an unexpected confidence led me on to where I could attempt a descent to the left. To negotiate a ten-foot drop I took off my pack and placed it on the ledge below. It landed badly, took a bounce, and continued falling, crashing against rocks again and again until it disappeared into the mist. For an instant I knew what a body must look like in a mountain fall. I quickly pulled myself together and carefully eased my way down. As I descended, snow turned back to rain and the storm abated. I was able to retrieve my pack, slightly damaged but essentially intact.

The sun came out abruptly. Fat marmots, barely able to waddle after a summer's diet of rich herbage, kept me company, their comical presence lightening my step after my scare. Soon I realized that at some point I had crossed an invisible line, from pine and beech forests into the drier, warmer Mediterranean zone.

Eleven hours of mountain walking brought me finally to the hamlet of Roure, a "perched village" built on a balcony high above the valley of the Tinée River. Such perched villages are a legacy from Italy, a stone's throw away over the crest of the Alps. Houses with roofs of maroon slate piled up vertically, one on top of the other, built for defense and for the husbanding of scarce flat agricultural land. In this remote village I had to knock on doors to find the keeper of the key to let me into a traveler's hostel. I eventually found a cheerful woman who questioned me about the mountain, the storm, and my reason for arriving so late. I told her only that I felt utterly thankful for the day, for my life, and for the chance to know the harsh beauty of Mercantour's mountains. I had the hostel to myself this evening, and celebrated with bread, butter, and a tin of ravioli; such simple fare seemed a banquet.

In bed I thought of other hostels, where I had found the company of fellow walkers. In one, a Basque brother and sister, both in their late teens, had come to Mercantour to compare the Alps with their own familiar Pyrenees mountains. In another, two women had fled Paris for a week of fresh air; each carried in her backpack a bottle of very good, expensive wine, which they shared with me at our

A draped sleeping bag warms an overnight visitor to the Vallée des Merveilles. Deserving of its name, the Valley of Marvels is adorned with ancient petroglyphs.

communal dining table. And above all I thought of the sad, pensive old man who had lost his son in a mountaineering accident; he was walking "to both remember…and to forget."

Morning proved a balm as I chose to go slowly through the Mediterranean world, letting ample time guide my descent of 2,000 feet toward the valley of the Tinée. Flowers grew taller and insects buzzed richer in their variety. I dawdled to take in the small, seemingly insignificant parts of the landscape. Hour after hour of sunshine warmed the earth and forest. Snout-nosed beetles, long-legged spiders, chirping crickets, a brown mantis with harlequin back, giant bumblebees, a hummingbird moth, ripe berries, hazelnuts underfoot, the scent of lavender—all caught my attention along the way.

A harmless four-foot water snake accompanied me downhill for a few yards. Along a low stone wall I crept up to observe an 18-inch common green lizard. Sunbathing, this diminutive, hunched dinosaur ignored me until the last instant. Then it leapt into the underbrush and disappeared. Wild fruit trees shaded my way through this dreamscape until I finally emerged onto the valley floor, took off my

. . . .

clothes, and plunged into the clear, icy Tinée River. Huge tumbled boulders had created a natural semicircular dam, which formed a deep pool.

To the east of my swimming hole the town of St.-Martin-Vésubie stands near the geographic center of the park, at a crossroads for tourists driving to Mercantour from the Riviera and Provence. Its narrow streets lie in shadow most of each day, but in the mornings bright market stalls pop up, with vendors selling cheese, honey, flowers, beets, salami, braids of garlic, and freshly baked bread. Between the tables and stalls runs a stone-lined channel with glistening water rushing the full length of the town, past steps and doorways. I watched the local children, shouting gleefully, place bright flower petals in the water and then race downstream after the flecks of color—but the petals always seemed to get away. The town's heavy stone churches and countless Madonna chapels give a nod to nearby Italy. This Italian inheritance came across to me vividly when buying a small jar of thyme-scented honey. The salesman spoke with high-trilled Italian *r*'s, not the back-of-the-throat *r* of standard French.

St.-Martin-Vésubie once functioned as an important way station along the "Route du Sel"—the salt route—a vital economic link between France and Italy from the Middle Ages up to the 19th century. From the salty marshes of France's Mediterranean coast came sacks of the coveted white crystals, carried on the backs of thousands of mules each year, over the Alps and into northern Italy's populated river valleys. Now this ancient Alpine link between the two countries has a modern twist. The Parc National du Mercantour has formed an alliance with Italy's Parco Naturale Alpi Marittime (Natural Park of the Maritime Alps), another protected mountain realm abutting Mercantour at the international border. Ecologists like to speak of "mountains without borders," and here such a slogan will actually become reality. Though less than half the size of Mercantour, the Italian park will add size and resilience to the region's biodiversity and mountain way of life. By 2005 the two are expected to merge to create the continent's first "European park." Over 375 miles of walking trails within Mercantour alone are revitalizing the ancient salt route, traditional pilgrimage trails, royal hunting paths, and military routes—a network that gives hikers and naturalists free access between the two countries.

Another kind of creature has crossed the border recently. The Italian wolf

When the big ones are biting out in the middle of the Ubayette, local anglers haul out their 18-foot fishing rods and cast their lines for trout.

(*Canis lupus italicus*) migrated naturally from the Apennine Mountains to Italy's western Alps and over into France. An estimated 20 wolves are found in Mercantour, though they are extremely wary and rarely seen. Even these few wolves face resistance from shepherds and hunters. Along village roadsides I saw hastily painted graffiti: *"Vive le loup!"* and *"A bas le loup!"* (Down with the wolf!), reflecting the emotional debate between supporters, who applaud the wolf's return to France, and detractors, who fear that a growing wolf population will threaten flocks and quarry.

Mercantour's most spectacular inhabitants are its three species of ungulates. Noble ibex, emblematic of high mountains from Europe to the Himalaya, with tall, arcing horns, are known as *bouquetin* in France and number about 700 in the park. Mouflon, relatives of North America's bighorn wild sheep, command rocky slopes and pinnacles. Once they were found solely on the islands of Corsica and Sardinia, but hunters introduced them to mainland Europe for sport in the 19th century.

First recorded as a Roman fortified camp in the 12th century, the pink-hued village of Roubion floats on a dark rock cliff at the edge of Mercantour. Above its cobblestone streets stand the remains of a four-turreted feudal castle.

Today about 600 mouflon survive in the park but are masters at evasion. The only sightings I made were of pert, young chamois, with their short horns curving backward from the forehead. Eight thousand chamois roam Mercantour's mountains, and I had several encounters, yet each time I was startled anew by their unmistakable cry, somewhere between a screech and a wheeze.

In high places and when crossing passes I searched the skies with binoculars for one of nature's greatest fliers, a rare giant known as the bearded vulture, or lammergeier. With wingspans of nearly ten feet, these unique birds, representing an evolutionary niche between eagle and vulture, soar and glide, then plummet in a

After summering in the mountains high above the village of St.-Martin-Vésubie, a statue of the Madonna is borne back to the valley in a traditional procession. The figure, a copy of a 12th-century original, is kept in the mountaintop sanctuary of La Madone de Fenestre from July to September.

blur to a new eating site. Up to 80 percent of their nutrition comes from bones, ligaments, and tendons of the remains of wild and domestic animals. Lammergeiers once thrived throughout much of southern Europe. But in the 19th century the birds suffered slow extermination, largely due to the misconception that they were ferocious, capable of killing sheep and carrying off human babies. In the Alps, hunters killed the last one in 1913.

Today lammergeiers exist in a natural state in the Pyrenees, Corsica, and Greece. In 1986 a team of international experts began releasing them in the Alps at four sites—in Austria, Switzerland, Italy, and France—and in 1993 the program extended to Mercantour, where fewer than ten individuals survive in the wild.

The glittering afternoon of my fourth day in Mercantour brought me through upland terrain, far above La Madone de Fenestre in the park's eastern sector, to a stand of larch, among Europe's oldest living trees. Their gnarled trunks carry rings of memory over a thousand years old. Along with these deciduous conifers grow pine trees whose seeds are sometimes deposited by birds in the most unlikely places, where it proves impossible for them to grow straight and tall. I saw one pine, stunted but stable, growing horizontally out of a cliff face. Nearby on the same cliff pecked an uncommon bird with the humdrum English name "wallcreeper." Living up to the snow line, it does indeed spend much time on cliff walls searching for insects. But in flight, dipping and fluttering like an enormous wild butterfly, it dazzles with flashes of white, gray, and black; brilliant patches of red, dotted with white spots, decorate rounded wings.

That night, camping out again, I witnessed a rising gibbous moon emerge from the side of a mountain, as if Earth herself were giving birth to an egg. An eagle owl, Europe's largest owl, sent a deep, far-ranging "boo-hu, boo-hu" through the late evening forest.

The following day I carried on into the Vallée des Merveilles (Valley of Marvels) near Mercantour's easternmost border to experience the park's grandest scenery, its most varied flora, and a startling prehistoric inheritance from the Bronze Age (1800-1500 B.C.): over 36,000 mysterious stone inscriptions and petroglyphs—carvings of bulls, horns, knives, circles, geometric designs, and strange, haunting images of humans.

By arrangement I linked up with Jean-Marie Cevasco, a park "ranger," though the title falls far short of his full functions as *garde-moniteur*—educator, policeman, outreach administrator, guide, photographer, field biologist, and historian. Fit and wiry, with dark hair, sharp features, and intense eyes, he led me to the ancient sanctuary, where shallow relief carvings on vast flat stones line both sides of the high,

The town of St.-Martin-Vésubie, dating from the 12th century, takes advantage of its steep streets and gravity to channel water downhill in an aqueduct system.

narrow Vallée des Merveilles. On our way we met an elderly white-haired woman crouched beside a glyph, floppy canvas hat protecting her from the sun's sharp rays here at 7,200 feet. Jean-Marie greeted her as a good friend. She introduced herself to me as Françoise, "a Bronze Age fool," jocular reference to her more than 20 years among the giant rocks and terraced plateaus. An amateur prehistorian and hunter of inscriptions, she was fascinated by the stylized carvings created with simple tools of bronze and copper—the numinous bulls, the endlessly repeated horns, the tens of thousands of images that seemed by their placement at its foot to honor a central mountain.

"There!" she pointed up to the right of the valley. "See his domed, rounded head? That is Mont Bégo. That's *him,* a god-mountain and center of the universe for these ancient, forgotten people."

Jean-Marie urged me on toward the 8,924-foot-high Mont des Merveilles, just

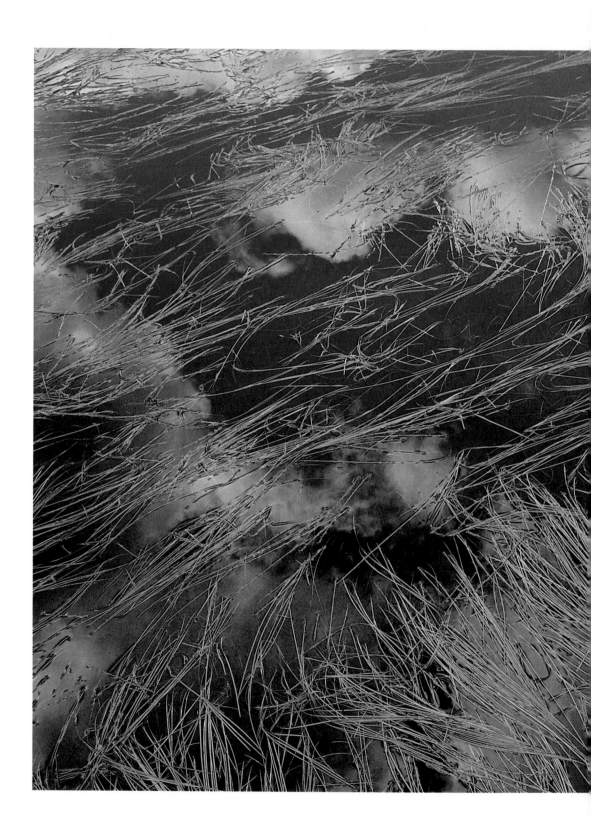

Nature lies at ease in Lac Vert, an aquatic grass-lined lake in the park. Officials find themselves caught between those who want to encourage tourism and others who insist that too much visitation is a threat. For years ecologists and visitors have battled over allowing such activities as mountain biking, hiking, and off-road driving.

west of the 9,423-foot Mont Bégo. Above us it rose to an immense stony spire; at eye level blotches of lime yellow and orange lichen contrasted sharply with green and pale blue-green rocks. Carvings spread across smooth reddish stones all around us; among them was the park's largest bull. Though its head measures only four inches tall, its thin horns extend for ten feet on either side, the whole configuration enclosing a standing human form, a trident-like weapon, and depictions of finely carved knives.

Scholars undertook serious study of the petroglyphs in the late 1800s, explained Jean-Marie, and a century of researchers have ventured explanations for the symbolic meaning of certain glyphs. "A closed circle stands for woman, or birth. The bull represents the masculine force in nature, power and plenty. A pair of horns with the tips touching symbolizes male and female unity. Horns that emerge from a bull's head in zigzag fashion stand for lightning. Bulls, horns, and weapons appearing together denote strength. Or so they say." Jean-Marie remains skeptical about any final interpretations of the images made by these mysterious people who left almost nothing else to offer clues—no tools, no weapons, no houses. To underscore the point, he explained that the real name of the Vallée des Merveilles is the Vallée des Mystères (Valley of Mysteries). "The French mistranslated the original Italian name," he said, "which meant something closer to 'strange and mysterious' than 'marvelous.'"

In addition to Bronze Age inscriptions, carved graffiti have accumulated on the mountainsides over hundreds of years—crosses and churches from the Middle Ages, and, somewhat later, houses, boats and sails, soldiers, shepherds' signs, military markings, names of outlaws and visitors. Incised dates stand out: 1546, 1609, 1829, 1881, 1906. The last, inscribed as "Bresso 1906," forms a bridge to the present. The Bresso of that time is a forebear of Signore Bresso, who now runs a taxi service bringing tourists to the Vallée des Merveilles.

Later in the day Jean-Marie led the way across a final stretch of flowery fields to a cabin used by the gardes-moniteurs. Here he introduced me to his colleagues, two men and a woman, while he prepared something on the stove. He soon came over and said, "Try this," placing before me a bowl filled with steaming amber liquid. "Mountain tea!" he declared, and the others joined us around the table. Jean-Marie's special concoction was an infusion of mountain thyme, veronica, and génépi, the herb also called wormwood that is famous for flavoring absinthe. Delicious, slightly sweet, vaguely medicinal. I was cold and worn out, but this brought me back to life.

After the tea I said good-bye to Jean-Marie, and in fading gray light struck out from the cabin to stand silently in the presence of Mont Bégo and Mont des

Recalling the time when Mercantour teemed with unfettered wildlife, a statue of a chamois perches high above the cliffside village of Roubion. Today some 600 chamois and wild sheep still populate the mountains.

Following pages: Wisps of clouds give way to delicate morning light above Lac Long Supérieur, which lies protected by the surrounding Alps.

Merveilles. They had towered protectively above those long-ago worshipers who honored the mountains with their myriad images. Today they help give sanctuary to plants, birds, and mammals. This sheltering arc of the southern Alps permitted ancient rhythms of life to carry on and stood as a bastion against the encroaching world of commerce and technology. A strong wind pushed me on my way as I left behind my deepest hope that education, growing public awareness, and the care of the gardes-moniteurs would let the mountains continue to do so forever.

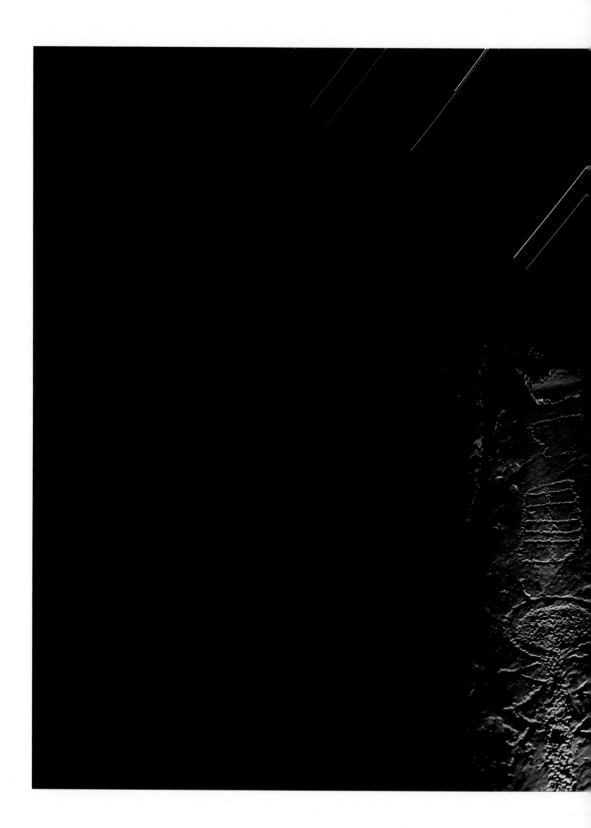

Thousands of years after Bronze Age artists carved some 30,000 petroglyphs into Mercantour's rocky hillsides, contemporary admirers have given them fanciful names. The "cosmonaut," also known as the "puppet with zigzag arms," stands guard over the Vallée des Merveilles in this two-hour exposure. Vandals have damaged many such carvings; one treasured stone was removed by helicopter.

Europe

Other National Parks of Note

Sareks National Park

Schiermonnikoog National Park

Białowieża National Park

Sareks National Park, Sweden

In 1909 Sweden created Europe's first national parks. One was Sareks, a wild zone of 760 square miles in the country's far north above the Arctic Circle. Its mountains, glaciers, windswept valleys, taiga, and marshy inland deltas abut neighboring parks to form the Lapponian Area, Western Europe's largest expanse of wilderness. Biologists consider Sareks to be of exceptional natural and aesthetic importance. This traditional homeland of the Saami (Lapp) people still sees reindeer herding, but the absence of roads and tourist facilities guarantees that just 2,000 visitors arrive each year.

Schiermonnikoog National Park, Netherlands

Like a string of beads, the five main West Frisian Islands form a low-lying barrier between the North Sea and the Netherlands coast. Between islands and coast lies the Waddenzee, a saltwater tidal delta of shallows and mudflats that forms northern Europe's most important wetland environment. Schiermonnikoog, eastern anchor of these Dutch islands, became a national park in 1989 to protect tens of thousands of indigenous and migratory birds, especially ducks, terns, geese, and waders. The park, though only 21 square miles, consists of dunes, marshes, grasslands, and pine woods. Large numbers of birders and nature lovers come each year, but no cars are allowed.

Białowieża National Park, Poland

Once a hunting reserve for Polish kings and Russian tsars, the park compasses 39 square miles of primeval woodland in the heart of Poland's Białowieża Forest. This mixed broadleaf and evergreen forest is considered the most important in all lowland Europe, in part for its great age (10,000 years) and remarkable biodiversity. The park's many large mammals include moose, red deer, and, rarest of all, wisent,

Doñana National Park

Pindos and Vikos-Aóös National Parks

or European bison. Smaller relatives of the American bison, the wisent were saved from near extinction in the 1920s and are now thriving in the park.

Doñana National Park, Spain

This 300-square-mile Biosphere Reserve and UNESCO World Heritage site, in southern Spain's Andalusia region, touches the Atlantic along 15 miles of coastline and takes in the estuary, vast marshlands, and adjacent plains of the wide Guadalquiver River. Famous for varied biotopes, Doñana includes scrubland, lagoons, sand dunes, beaches, and swamps. On the migration route between Europe and West Africa, the wetlands annually welcome some half a million birds—up to 365 species—including spoonbills and flamingos. Forests, heath, caper, and brush provide cover for threatened Spanish lynx and 29 other types of mammals. Popular Doñana receives a quarter of a million visitors annually, but all must enter the park with local guides.

Pindos and Vikos-Aóös National Parks, Greece

Like a backbone arcing from north to south through mainland Greece, the Pindos Mountains encompass two of Greece's six national parks, both near the Albanian border. Ranging in elevation from 4,000 to 8,000 feet, the deep valleys and precipitous mountains are covered with forests of beech, fir, and pine. A particularly dramatic feature here is the eight-mile-long Vikos Gorge, cutting a thousand feet beneath exposed limestone faces. Pindos is the sole park in Europe where wolves, brown bears, boars, and lynx coexist, while cliffside monasteries and abandoned stone villages speak of earlier inhabitants.

AFRICA

Africa

Kruger National Park

Douglas Bennett Lee

On the wall of a museum in South Africa's Kruger National Park hangs a lion skin with three knife holes. The weapon hangs beneath it, a short-bladed knife wielded in one hand by a desperate ranger as he was dragged, grasped in the lion's mouth. The ranger, Harry Wolhuter by name, struck the animal's heart and jugular vein, and the lion dropped him and went off to die. Despite his terrible wounds, Harry managed to climb a tree to escape the lion's partner. Nearly fainting, he strapped himself to a branch with his belt until help arrived.

Beside a gravel road in a remote section of the park, bronze plaques and a small limb of the tree are set in concrete to memorialize the drama. Present-day ranger Leon Serfontein leads walking safaris here, always with a degree of delight. He marvels at the thought of what happened that night in 1903. "Imagine smelling that lion's breath! Imagine feeling for your knife! Think of what goes through your head!"

It's especially thought-provoking when you've walked up to a lion kill just that morning. We'd heard a pride roaring late the night before as we lay beneath mosquito nets in thatch-roofed A-frame huts at the safari's simple base camp. Not long after dawn, as we set off on foot along the same stream where Wolhuter was attacked, two male lions called in deep, guttural growls. During a stop for a breakfast snack, we'd seen vultures rising in the distance; then, as we hiked farther, we smelled the stench of death.

Drag marks and a bare brown patch marked the spot where the lions had made their meal. Dung beetles worked industriously, rolling up the last of the victim's

Tracking expertise and bush experience enable guides to drive visitors safely into a Cape buffalo herd in a protected African wilderness famed for close-up encounters.

Preceding pages: Fast and focused, lionesses race over grasslands in Kruger National Park. South Africa's biggest and oldest sanctuary showcases Africa's "big five"—lion, leopard, elephant, rhino, and buffalo—amid a host of lower-profile wild denizens.

stomach contents. The other ranger with our group, Abel Legari, picked up a scrap of skin and black hair. "Zebra," he said. "Last night. Those lions we heard."

Most of the 650,000 annual visitors to Kruger see lions only through the windows of their cars and RVs. Rules are strict in this park, as they must be to prevent the mayhem that could occur with so many tourists driving themselves through a land so vast and varied. Stretching 236 miles north to south and an average of 33 east to west, Kruger is an 8,000-square-mile chunk of wild Africa—a place nearly the size of Wales or New Jersey. Fenced on all sides, it envelops 16 ecozones ranging from low mountains to lush river valleys to open savannas, from thorny scrub to grasslands to thick forests, encompassing climates from temperate to tropical.

Animals still dominate here, and the park's fauna represents a zoological smorgasbord: The year 2000 birder's list stands at 507 spotted in the park—nearly a third of the species in Africa. Its 147 types of mammals range from elephants to elephant shrews; its 94 kinds of reptiles from Nile crocodiles weighing a ton to pythons nearly 20 feet long. Add to that 33 types of amphibians and 49 fish.

To protect both animals and tourists, visitors are allowed to step out of their cars only at designated scenic points and picnic areas, where signs inform them that they do so at their own risk. By sundown everyone must be safely ensconced within one of Kruger's overnight rest camps, fenced against wild intruders.

Everyone, that is, except people on one of the park's walking safaris. Introduced in the late 1970s, these foot safaris were seen as boldly adventurous innovations, particularly for an organization famous for resisting change—the oldest and largest national park of a deeply conservative country. In the two decades that followed the innovation of walking safaris, greater changes swept the nation, reaching even into the wilds of this flagship institution, which since its founding in 1898 has been a living, evolving symbol of what South Africa stands for.

Abel Legari is a citizen of the new South Africa and a member of the Tswana tribe. With Leon, he led six of us hikers, representing five different countries, on a two-day bushwhacking odyssey through varied terrain. On one of the mornings we all watched anxiously as Leon warily approached a thornbush thicket, where we could hear the moist sounds of chewing. Both rangers carried .458-caliber big-game rifles, now held at port arms to fire warning shots—or, if necessary, to kill a charging animal. The last thing the rangers wanted to do was shoot, but they needed to know we were protected as we hiked past.

Leon gave an all clear for us to approach, and, peering into shadows, we could make out what was left of a zebra's torn haunch and bloodied rib cage. Whatever had been chewing on them had vanished. "Could have been a lion, a leopard, or a hyena," Leon said. "We'll never know."

In our two days together, we also crept near enough to a white rhino cow and calf to make out the youngster's nubbin of a horn and soft baby features as it suckled; witnessed jackals playing tag with sharp-horned impala who chased them back; stood admiring the bucolic peace of a lush, vine-hung swale just as a scaly crocodilian head broke the water's green surface. Our base camp offered rustic comfort: Running water, showers heated by wood fires, comfortable bunks, and a lamplit open-air dining hall where the cook, a native of Mozambique, seasoned four-course dinners with savory Portuguese flavors. The camp's fence was low enough for a lion or leopard to spring across easily, and we carried flashlights when we walked to our huts in the dark.

A landmark of African conservation (map), Kruger's 8,000 square miles of fenced wilderness grew out of Sabi Game Reserve, where the Boer Transvaal Republic banned hunting in 1898.

Following pages: A breeding herd of elephant cows and calves hustles across a sand road in the hinterland. Most visitors drive themselves over hundreds of miles of park roads, witnessing through their windshields a natural world managed but not controlled.

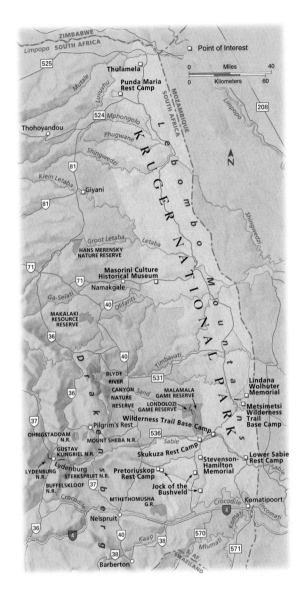

At sunrise, peacefulness ruled the broad, open plain before us as a line of wildebeest loped out of the dawn. Beyond them the sun slowly rose over the Lebombo Mountains—long, stony ridges running the length of Kruger's eastern border—ramparts against Mozambique just over their crests and the unquiet, uncontrollable Africa beyond.

As we set off on our day's safari, herds of hartebeest, impala, and zebra dropped their heads to graze when we stopped walking. "This is the Africa I dreamed of when

I was a kid," said Leon, grinning. "They can see all around, they're not afraid, they let us into their space."

He narrowed his eyes. "If I were a cheetah, I'd come and live here."

After three days of splendid isolation, Skukuza had all the bustle of a small town. Home to a third of Kruger's 2,900 employees, it is also the largest of the park's seven main rest camps, with beds for some 1,000 tourists. The lodgings range from luxurious group houses to round, thatch-roofed cabins called rondavels to inexpensive campsites. On my visit, menus in the high-ceilinged, darkly paneled central dining room ran to colonial-era tastes, with curries, stews, and excellent roasts, while the cafeteria served meat pies of antelope and buffalo.

The town comes to life between 4:30 and 6:00 a.m., when engines start up and cars head out into Kruger's wild lands, threaded by 540 miles of tarred roads and another 840 of gravel. My own one-day drive out from Skukuza barely touched the park's immensity, but it was still filled with surprises and went something like this:

4:30 a.m.—Into the park before dawn. The Milky Way is lustrous overhead, the Southern Cross a jeweled crucifix. The air is sharp with the aromatic vegeta-

In a predator's paradise, hunting cats are never hunted, and leopards (opposite) are less elusive than kin outside the park. Researchers identify individuals by facial spots as distinctive as fingerprints. In thick bush, one of Kruger's 2,000 lions lies all but invisible (above).

Following pages: Defying gravity, a series of valves in a giraffe's neck veins stop blood from rushing to its brain at the vulnerable moment of drinking. Oxpeckers groom the giraffe, feeding on ticks and other parasites, and often warn of a predator's approach.

tion of the lowveld, as this part of Africa is called, a near-sea level plain stretching almost uninterrupted toward Mozambique and the Indian Ocean.

4:45 a.m.—A solitary lion slouches up the road, eyes gleaming like yellow flames in our headlights. He walks past, perhaps five feet away. He stops and sprays a bush, marking his territory, then fades into the gloaming. We are quieted by the sideways glance he gives us, eye-to-eye, head level with ours.

5:00 a.m.—The sky is coral over the Lebombo Mountains. A band of kudu blocks the road, tall-shouldered, smoke gray antelope with spiral horns atop noble profiles. They stare, then bound away not so much through the brush as over it, fleet messengers of dawn. *Continued on p. 122*

*A feathered gang of more
than 500 species swells
Kruger's avian roster.
Flocking to a rich variety
of habitats provided by
16 ecozones within park
borders, birds seek out
favored climates from
tropical to temperate.
Some make permanent
homes, others only
seasonal stops on
migrations between
Asia and Europe.
A yellowbilled hornbill
(opposite) lives here
year-round, joined in
the rainy season by
whitefronted bee-eaters
(right) that pass the dry
winter months across
the Equator in the balmy
Mediterranean climes
of North Africa.*

Recalling a line from Tennyson, "Nature, red in tooth and claw," age-old enemies engage in life-and-death combat as one among countless daily dramas unfolds on Kruger's expansive stage. Separated from her pride, a lioness turns to face her tormentors in a scrap over food and territory. The hyenas' united front may outmatch her size and strength in a story often played out but rarely witnessed.

5:45 a.m.—Clear sunlight floods the low-topped, thorny bush, warming a tribe of mongoose busily hunting the road's verge. They're as hyperactive as ferrets, as ruthless as pirates in their scavenging.

6:00 a.m.—We take a winding side road up a kopje, one of the rounded, rocky hills that rise like islands from the lowveld's rolling green sea. At its top we step from our car and gaze out at the spot where the ashes of Col. James Stevenson-Hamilton, a park founder, and his wife, Hilda, were scattered across the land. Made warden in 1902, four years after the original reserve was declared, Stevenson-Hamilton ruled for 44 years. The tribal peoples he moved off the newly established sanctuary gave him the name "Skukuza," a Zulu term meaning "he who sweeps clean." That's how the world seemed when Stevenson-Hamilton told them they could no longer run cattle or hunt within the reserve. The name was not meant as a term of endearment.

The fresh, scented air of the park is never empty of birdsong. Big birds are out now, vultures, hawks, and eagles searching for rising currents. One drops, hurtling toward a songbird that dives into the canopy. Both disappear and the green sea never blinks, as serene in the early light as if nothing had ever happened.

7:00 a.m.—A white rhino grazes just off the road, one of 1,800 in the park. The world's greatest concentration of the prehistoric creatures is a triumph of conservation, for the rhino had been hunted to local extinction in pre-park days, then was reintroduced in 1961.

9:00 a.m.—We're tracing a route taken in the late 1800s by wagoneers linking the goldfields to the west with ports on the Indian Ocean. Theirs was a rough-and-tumble life immortalized in South Africa's all-time adventure novel, *Jock of the Bushveld*, a man-and-his-dog story remembered in plaques and place-names along the road.

Malaria, the disease that helped keep the lowveld wild, is still endemic in the park, and visitors are advised to take preventive medication. I learned the importance of taking it regularly a month after one of my visits, when shakes, chills, nausea, and a 104°F fever landed me in a Johannesburg hospital.

12:00 p.m.—The bush is quiet in the heated hush of noon. Most animals doze deep in shade, but not the ubiquitous impala, 160,000 strong in the park, broadest base of the carnivores' food pyramid. They give us no more than a glance from a few feet away, barely parting to let us through. This year's young scamper in nursery crèches, carefree for the moment while the meat eaters sleep.

Some hunters don't take a midday recess. A yellowbilled hornbill crunches a scorpion that hangs limp, claws dangling, from a bill the size and shape of a banana.

2:00 p.m.—We set off down a gravel road near the park's perimeter after a picnic at Pretoriuskop. In the next three hours we meet only two cars but make a full

Animals emerge out of wood at a craft stand on a main route to Kruger. Under programs with neighboring communities, the park provides artists with training and co-op markets.

stop for a column of Matabele ants. The fierce, inch-long warriors are returning from a raid on a termite nest, mandibles crammed with soft white prey. I leave them in peace, because their sting is said to be as painful as a wasp's.

3:00 p.m.—Where an early trading post has been partly restored, I break park rules by walking out of the designated area to the park's fence, to look out to neighboring pastures and houses. I can hear a radio playing, distant voices, then the rumble of an electric train on tracks beside the fence.

5:00 p.m.—Back on tarmac, nearing Skukuza, I drive slowly up to a knot of vehicles. A driver leans from his window, smile on his face, and points out two lions all but hidden in a thicket.

6:00 p.m.—Baboons on a bridge are amusing a crowd, but one family is dismayed when a big male leaps into the bed of their truck and rifles through their groceries, baring huge canine teeth. I think of a scene at Lower Sabie Rest Camp when baboons raided fridges along a line of rondavels at dawn. One couple stood recording it on video, while the baboons ran with armfuls of fruit and packaged food, strewing trash in their wake—a challenge of primate primacy.

. . . .

6:30 p.m.—Into the gated safety of Skukuza just as the flags of South Africa and the national parks slide down their poles. Fires burn at cookouts, parents in folding chairs watch children play. Crickets, frogs, and cicadas start up an evening chorus, joined by bell-gong soundings of fruit bats, like clocks chiming in thin air.

It's only after full dark that the thrilling whoop of hyenas sounds out of the utter blackness beyond. Far off a lion roars, another answers, and Africa lets us know where we really are.

Kruger's wealth of wildlife plays a role beyond entertainment. Behind the scenes at Skukuza's veterinary corrals, white rhinos await shipment to zoos on other continents. Alongside them are black rhinos repatriated to Africa from the United States and Germany; they will be reintroduced to the Kruger wild.

Park Veterinarian Douw Groebler tugs affectionately on the three-foot, mud-caked horn of a male, wagging the rhino's head. "This bull had no future in America. White rhinos are grass-eaters, they're easy to feed, but black rhinos are browsers. If they don't have the right fodder, they won't breed. There are only 1,300 in the world, so we've got to keep the gene pool as broad as possible. Here he's got a future."

Unlike their highly endangered cousins, white rhinos are very nearly in surplus in the park. But an even bigger problem has faced the park for many years, a problem as big as any get: What do you do with too many elephants?

The drive north is a journey into elephant country. First come the mid-park plains, grasslands, and savannas resembling East Africa's well-known vistas, with the greatest antelope herds grazing the best, most open country. As with any spot in Kruger, you may see elephants here. But north of that, across the Tropic of Capricorn in tropical Africa, a forest of mopane trees grows gradually higher as you get closer to the Equator, and you come into lands the elephants own.

One morning here, I heard a far-off trumpet that put my hair up, like a bray out of a Jurassic jungle. Soon enough, sure enough, a big bull lumbered up the road toward me. He slowed as he came close, explored the alternative of walking off the road but finally came right at me in a mock charge, ears out and flapping, trumpeting to wake the dead. He lifted a foreleg and shook a foot at me, two car-lengths away. He certainly raised my heart rate, but when I sat quietly, motor off, he hurried off-road to hide his head behind a bush until I drove on.

Wildebeest, impala, giraffe, zebra, and other animals gather cheek by jowl to drink at shrinking water holes during the dry season, from May to September.

A toothy grin from a Nile crocodile reveals its dinner of hinged terrapin. The reptile lords, weighing a ton or more and growing to 18 feet, may haunt any patch of water deep and dark enough to hide their bulk. Rivers flowing from mountains west of Kruger nourish fertile valleys year-round. As the millennium turned, heavy rains raised the rivers to overflowing, causing floods of near-biblical dimensions.

The dangers and dilemma with Kruger's elephants lie not in solitary bulls but in breeding herds of cows and calves. I sat endlessly one afternoon as mothers and aunts herded young ones across the road in front of me, hurrying them over open ground by a river to tarry in thicker roadside forest. A park maintenance person, used to such roadblocks, showed up, assessed the situation, then gunned his engine and came forward. A cow challenged him but turned with a peal of anger and ran through the bush in my direction. This time I switched my engine on, ready to run…but quietly. Thankfully I didn't see her again, but I could hear the rage of her passage, shrieks and crashing branches, as she moved by like a storm.

Managers estimate that the park can sustain about 8,000 elephants. Many times, culls have been carried out to control their numbers, most recently in 1993. Culling is an ugly business, the shooting of entire breeding herds of cows and calves after darting them with tranquilizers, sparing only a few very young ones for zoos and other parks. No one looks forward to culling again, but no other solution has been found. The millennium began with 8,800 Kruger elephants.

Dr. L.E.O. Braack, head of research, tells me how management goals have evolved. "The park started with a nearly pristine environment. At first, managers went for stasis, trying to preserve everything just as it was. Now we know that nature isn't static. We manage for heterogeneity and flux, to encourage biodiversity."

In the past, water holes were established where water wasn't supposed to be, leading to overgrazing and lopsided populations. Now many have been closed. Drought and fire are allowed to work their natural cycles in trimming excess. "But elephants are one species that doesn't die off in drought cycles," Dr. Braack says. They have no natural enemies, so they predominate until damage to the environment raises the chilling specter of mass slaughters.

Alien invaders pose a low-profile but destabilizing threat to the park's natural equilibrium. Plants from other continents crowd out indigenous species. Thick growths of prickly pear from America's Southwest kill all competition. Lantana is a pretty South American weed whose juices can kill cattle or anything else that eats it, including us.

Bovine tuberculosis came into Cape buffalo herds from domestic cows on the park's borders. Transmitted to lions and other predators, it was spread further afield

A park-bred white rhino—square-lipped ray of hope for the endangered rhino population—thrives in a region where the creature was extinct before reintroduction began in 1961.

Following pages: Troublesome king of the African bush, a bull elephant strides over land heavily browsed by some of his 8,800 kin—considered too many for Kruger to sustain.

by scavengers, including vultures, who then transported it as far as they fly. The disease is entrenched only in the southern portion of the park, and there is ongoing discussion of a fence to divide north from south.

Policing poachers has been a never ending task since the park's beginning. But the nature of poaching changed in the 1980s, from subsistence hunters taking meat to well-armed bands in four-wheel-drives hunting ivory and rhino horn. Antipoaching measures have changed to cope. Gun battles killed a number of poachers and wounded a ranger. But park officers have found since that local intelligence is the best weapon. "The park's too big to patrol with 250 rangers, you can see that," said agent Frikkie Roussow over a helicopter's headset, as Kruger unrolled beneath our feet. "We have a network of informers in the villages. This year we've confiscated two weapons in the park, 23 outside it. We've been much more effective proactive than reactive. We're actually not an antipoaching unit. We're anti-environmental crimes."

Our flight today was, well, reactive, looking for a rhino skeleton to match DNA of a horn confiscated in Pretoria from a visitor who bragged that he'd "found" it in Kruger. As if we were vultures on a kill, we spiraled down to whitish bones enough times to make my stomach churn. None were rhino. But the flight gave me a bird's-eye perspective beyond the park's borders, from the fence to the purple escarpment of the Drakensberg Mountains. Roads, fields, and small, tin-roofed houses fill the red-clay landscape, where black tribespeople under the apartheid regime were confined in marginal areas designated "homelands." Apartheid is gone, but the masses remain on Kruger's doorstep.

"South Africa is a strange country," says David Mabunda, Kruger's director. "You have first- and third-world conditions side by side." David's father was born in what is now the park. His grandfather was evicted in the early "forcible removals," very likely by Skukuza himself. Little or no compensation was paid. Black visitors to Kruger were the exception rather than the rule before Nelson Mandela walked off Robbens Island a free man. Kruger was itself an island—a white one run largely by Afrikaners. Blacks were not welcome.

"We had an enemy called apartheid," David says, a young daughter on his lap as he relaxes after hours in his office. "Like all black people, I was excluded from the park. Blacks were only appreciated in roles of servitude. I never thought I'd find myself at the helm of what I called the Last Paradise of Apartheid. It was like a club for people who all spoke the same language, drank the same beer, went to the same schools, and had the same likes and dislikes. We're changing that culture. Above all we must make peace with our communities. If we continue to manage parks as islands, we'll be driving toward extinction."

Bad-boy bulls flee a helicopter chasing them inside Kruger's fence, where they'll be shot for raiding neighboring fields. Three and a half million Africans live around the park, which courts their goodwill despite relations sometimes strained by animal escapees.

Like so many South Africans, David worked clandestinely against the apartheid regime. Was it true, I ask, that he ran ANC operatives—terrorists in the eyes of many whites, freedom fighters to many blacks—infiltrating from Mozambique through Kruger. David's pleasant smile doesn't change. "There were many entrance and exit routes from the country. Kruger was one of them."

A major change for Kruger is looming with its expansion into a "transfrontier park," merging with reserves in adjoining Zimbabwe and Mozambique. If plans go as hoped, the tri-national park will become the largest in the world, encompassing four to six million acres. Tricky issues of antipoaching, free passage, and sovereignty still must be worked out. But the merger would *Continued on p. 138*

· · · · · · ·

Feline fluidity of a leopard at rest (opposite) belies its lightning-quick reactions and temperament. At Londolozi, a private game ranch within Kruger's fences, five generations of leopards have grown up in the wild (right) without fear of humans. Descendants of two hand-reared orphan cubs, they open windows into lives seldom glimpsed.

Following pages: Midnight visitor to Mala Mala Game Reserve leaves only paw prints on its nightly rounds among cabins where guests lie sleeping. Private ranches inside the fences deliver a finely crafted mix of wildlife and tourist amenities.

double Kruger's available space, relieving pressure on elephants, among other species, for decades to come.

The tides of war lapped against the park's Lebombo Mountains during Mozambique's two decades of civil agony. Rangers watched firefights and attacks by helicopter gunships at the fence's edge and found stray rockets inside the park. Much of Mozambique's abundant wildlife was massacred during the rule of the AK-47. Now wildlife gets a new chance, and Kruger itself is reinvigorated.

Meanwhile on the park's western border, inside South Africa, the traditions of private hunting lodges and game ranches remain as venerable as Kruger itself. Several have dropped their fences to allow animals free passage, effectively adding themselves to the park. Most are world-class resorts, and in that first rank is Londolozi, famed for leopards and luxury.

Open at one end, its big A-frame lodge is actually an enormous tree house, built into the branches of a huge old fig and suspended, like much of the camp, along a river valley. Owner and guiding light, Dave Varty, is a man of visions, and he painted them vividly over an elegant Sunday dinner on the candlelit, tree-framed terrace.

"Let's move the fence to those mountains," he said, pointing a fork toward the distant Drakensbergs, "to the rivers' watershed. They're fundamental to Kruger's survival. The rivers link the mountains to the park. This country subordinated all to the industries of mining and agriculture. Now let it serve a new god."

Varty hopes that the new god is ecotourism, embraced by South Africa's current government as an economic power point, but still in its infancy. Londolozi mines the gold of the internationally well-heeled and uses part of the profits from jet-setting clientele to fund local schools, clinics, and artists. If expanding benefits can reach local communities, then marginal tribal lands can be revived as game land worth far more than tired farm fields. Londolozi's 30,000 acres, Varty points out, generate profits on a scale with Kruger's, which covers nearly 150 times more land.

Several generations of wild, free-ranging leopards became habituated to Londolozi's vehicles, and they show an indifference to us that is astounding in the most retiring of the big cats. We're not disturbing their lives; we're irrelevant. When a gobbet of meat drops beside me from a leopard feeding on a wildebeest calf wedged 20 feet over our heads, I know I'm close.

The past was palpably close on an afternoon at Thulamela, a partly restored Zimbabwe royal village that occupies a hilltop near the park's northern border. Today, elephant paths meander through the city's old fields, but when the city lived, from the 12th to the 17th centuries, councillors and kings held court under Thulamela's giant, spreading baobab trees. Three standing stones still guard the site. They were said to draw lightning, speak to the gods in times of crisis, and smell out witches to protect the royal household.

"High life" takes on new meaning at Londolozi's tree house lodge. The terrace overlooks a broad, forested riverbed where animals stroll and graze while guests drink and dine.

"These were Venda people," says Eddie Mahadas, a Venda himself. "We didn't have to read books to know about these people. We knew the stories before they put them in books." Venda elders hold ceremonies here every year, offering prayers and food and beer to ancestors who abide forever. "I can feel the presence of the ancestors," says Eddie, not as a figure of speech. His Zionist Christian Church allows room for traditional worship and Jesus Christ. "Our ancestors are real, they're visible. You must be taken to God by your ancestors."

The ancestors ruffled my hair with a breeze that blew up the cliff and over the low stone walls. Antelope trails crisscrossed the royal enclosure. The barking of baboons echoed off the rocks. It gave me a charge of hope, for the timelessness that is old Africa, and for the new South Africa that holds the future—and the past— in its hands. More than a heritage, Kruger is a living part of what's to come.

How long can all this last, I wondered. "The people still visit, the ancestors protect it, the stones of protection are here forever," Eddie smiled. "To infinity."

Eternal vigilance is the price of survival for impala on Kruger's savanna. Today's stewards of South Africa's wilderness jewel also remain alert to preserve its timeless values.

Other National Parks of Note

Mana Pools National Park

Serengeti National Park

Mount Kilimanjaro National Park

Mana Pools National Park, Zimbabwe

Ancient river bends, abandoned by the present-day Zambezi, create Mana Pools on the river's wide floodplain in northern Zimbabwe. During the dry season, from May to October, the pools become magnets for game and game enthusiasts. Campsites and a handful of lodges cater to international guests who fly or drive into the park. Organized foot safaris are popular, and canoe camping on the Zambezi gives adventurers access to the riverside's open game country in the wet season, when the park is closed to all other visitors.

Serengeti National Park/Masai Mara Reserve, Tanzania/Kenya

If one image of wild Africa dwells in our imagination, it's the rolling grasslands and free-roaming herds of the East African savanna. Tanzania's Serengeti National Park and Kenya's adjoining Masai Mara Reserve have no fence to divide their abundant wildlife, so herds still range across

them. The Serengeti, meaning "endless plains" in Masai, is actually one ecosystem. The Masai, cattle herders and fierce warriors, are allowed to keep cattle and to hunt in the Kenyan reserve, coexisting with tourists in one of Africa's most venerable and well-visited wild sanctuaries.

Mount Kilimanjaro National Park, Tanzania

The "House of God" to the Masai tribe, Africa's tallest peak—19,340-foot-high Mount Kilimanjaro—is also the highest in the world attainable without full alpine climbing equipment and skills. It's still no simple hike, and guides are necessary for the several-day-long adventure. Access is controlled and hikers must stay at designated rest huts. The route to the summit begins in a tropical rain forest, leads through heather dotted with cactus-like lobelias, and summits in a windswept, snowcapped tundra crowned with hanging glaciers just three degrees below the Equator.

Nouabalé-Ndoki National Park

Niokolo-Koba National Park

Tassili-n-Ajjer National Park

Nouabalé-Ndoki National Park, Congo

"Inaccessible" best describes one of Africa's wildest, most remote, and youngest parks, dedicated in 1993. Guarded by swamps, hills, and the unnavigable Ndoki River, the park remains largely pristine—even while surrounded by logging activities and under increasing pressure from Africa's human populations. Though not easy to see in the primeval terrain of rain forest and swamp, animal species that are abundant here though rare elsewhere—lowland gorillas, chimpanzees, and diminutive forest elephants—are increasingly at risk from poaching. Ecotourism may be part of the future here, but a visit today still entails a rugged expedition.

Niokolo-Koba National Park, Senegal

Located toward the outlying reaches of Africa's sub-Saharan flora and fauna, Niokolo-Koba harbors some of the continent's northernmost lions, elephants, and giraffes. Guests at the park's lodgings can take scheduled day drives into the park, or drive themselves, though only with a guide. They may camp wherever conditions allow, but must come prepared to be fully self-supporting. Forays into the less visited areas might bring scarce glimpses of wild dogs or chimpanzees.

Tassili-n-Ajjer National Park, Algeria

Rock paintings and carvings in the vast plateau known as the Tassili-n-Ajjer date back 8,000 years, to hunter-gatherers of a time when the Sahara was a lush garden watered by rivers long vanished. Later paintings record the presence of pastoral peoples who followed and those who came later still. Access is allowed only to guided individual or group tours—necessary to protect both the paintings and the tourists who come to a Sahara that's far less hospitable than in the early painters' days.

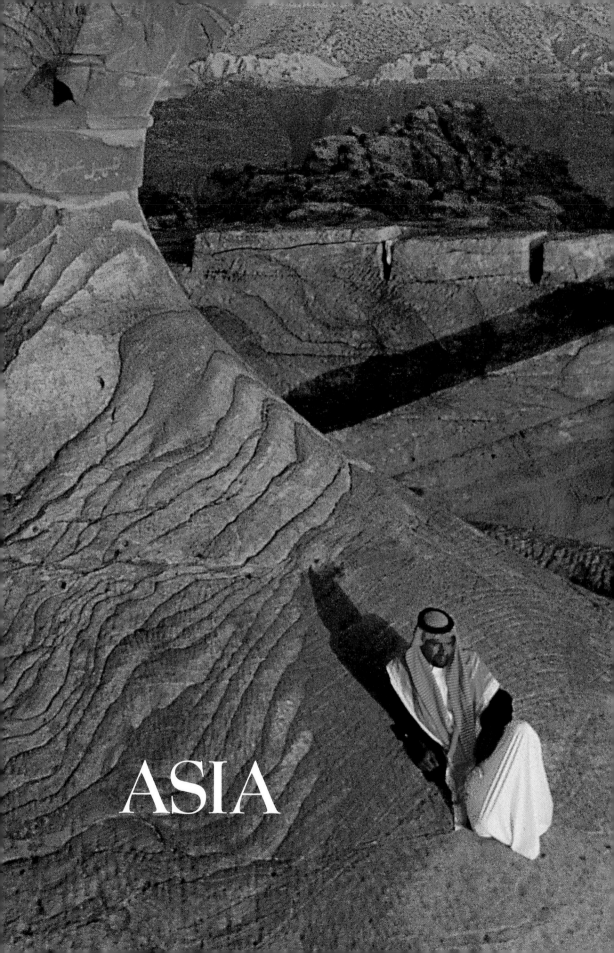

ASIA

Asia

Petra National Park

Text by Patrick Booz
Photographs by Annie Griffiths Belt

Leaving the noise of the world behind, I entered a canyon portal to the sanctuary city and strode down the winding mountain cleft, meandering past ancient water-courses and bas-relief sculptures of camels. At last, around a final turn, I stood face to face with the rock-cut grandeur of the Treasury. As my eyes moved up the 2,000-year-old facade, I saw a fan-tailed raven shoot across the skylight slit above, letting loose a single black feather that spiraled downward to land at my feet. This I took not as a portent, but as a punctuation mark to affirm that I had arrived at my goal. Pink clouds, backlit by a sunken sun, mirrored the colors of temples, tombs, and cliffs. A lone dog scurried away as I passed a line of immense tombs, each with an open doorway like the mouth of a death mask. A broad amphitheater, hewn from the mountain, seemed to melt into itself as the light dimmed. Turning back, I heard hooves clattering in the near-darkness of the canyon. The mystery seemed complete as walls closed in. Then, breaking the spell of intimacy, a Bedouin boy on a tiny donkey rode up, patted the beast's rump, and said, "Taxi, sir?"

Earlier that day, I had driven along the desert, south from Amman, Jordan's capital, then up and over the high rolling Shara mountains. Suddenly the sandstone range of Petra reared up like a massed pile of enormous geodes—rust, brown, and buff. I descended through the bustling tourist town of Wadi Musa, along crowded dusty streets with cars honking, past tawdry hotels and strips of souvenir stalls. This boomtown of 12,000 people, a much smaller Arab village just 20 years ago, would be my base for the next week. Wadi Musa, "Valley of Moses," derived its name from a spring above the town; biblical legend says water gushed forth when

Exquisite mosaics decorate the floor of a fifth-century Byzantine church near the city center. Beauty reigned as a hallmark of Petra even after the Romans sealed its doom by shifting trade routes away from it in the second century A.D.

Preceding pages: From the carved rooftop of a 2,000-year-old building known as Al Deir, the Monastery, a Bedouin surveys the realm of the Nabataeans, ancient builders of Petra.

Moses smote a stone with his staff. I soon learned that the Arabic word *wadi* could mean many things: the name of a town, the valley along a river course, an oasis by a wash, or a dry streambed.

Waking in darkness the following morning, I was at Petra's entrance gate by 6 a.m., opening time. I sped through the *siq*—the mountain cleft—stopping long enough to locate high up on the walls a frisky pair of Sinai rosefinches darting, swooping, and dashing in and out of crevices. These are Jordan's national bird. The male, through eons of evolution, has perfected its color to match the surrounding sandstone hues; the female, paler and browner, fits in just as well.

Energized by this sighting, I made a huge U-shaped detour to climb up the back side of Jebel al Khubtha, the eastern barrier massif that protected Petra city through the ages. I arrived at the top just in time to witness first light strike the Roman-style Collonaded Street; the vista below dispelled my first impression of Petra as a city merely of tombs and carved facades. Here instead was the heart of a once living entrepôt, a major caravan city of the Middle East that supported 30,000 people. Today the site reveals a monumental gateway, fountain ruins, a row of columns, grand stairways, tumbledown temples, and in-progress archaeological digs.

Since 1993 this legendary ancient city has been protected as Petra National Park, but even before that, in 1985, it had been added to UNESCO's list of World Heritage sites. Encompassing 350 square miles, the park actually comprises three areas: the ancient city sanctuary, an archaeological park of 100 square miles that contains more than 800 rock-carved monuments and includes the city, and a large buffer region surrounding these. "Petra is just at its start," says Aysar Akrawi, the buoyant, impassioned director of the Petra National Trust, which acts to preserve the park's archaeology and environment. "But already we are faced with the classic dilemma of tourism versus cultural preservation."

The 1994 peace treaty with Israel brought a huge jump in tourism, which is now Jordan's second largest industry. "Petra is an exceptionally fragile site," explains Aysar, "and we were unprepared for this onslaught. We are in a crisis situation, every day. Not one person in Jordan is properly trained in cultural resources management, so imagine! We need vision, and we need trained staff. What I fear is the blind development of tourism at the expense of our heritage."

That heritage is ancient and honored. The creators of the great city were Nabataeans, a tribe of nomads that came north and west out of the Arabian Peninsula around 400 B.C. These Bedouin—desert dwellers—knew the unforgiving desert realm intimately; wandering and herding was their essence. The Nabataeans added brigandage, but in time they realized that riches could be gained by protecting and taxing caravans, not robbing them of the luxury goods that crisscrossed deserts from the Red Sea to the Mediterranean, from Egypt to Babylon. Treasures included henna, spices, pearls, ivory, ostrich feathers, silk, precious metals, and above all frankincense and myrrh. The latter two—tree resin that was dried for incense and made into oils and perfumes—demanded high prices throughout the Roman world. Petra's strategic position on the land bridge between Africa and Asia proved ideal for channeling these items from place to place.

The Nabataean Empire, with many cosmopolitan crosscurrents coming from its mastery of the trade routes, reached its height between 100 B.C. and A.D. 100.

Petra National Park, a realm of desert, rock-carved monuments, and a "lost" city, encompasses 350 square miles in the southwestern region of Jordan.

Following pages: Carved from stone, the Monastery, like all of Petra, seems to grow from the cliffs that embrace it. Earthquakes, storms, and sand battered and partly obscured these structures, but it was the mists of time that eventually hid Petra from Western memory.

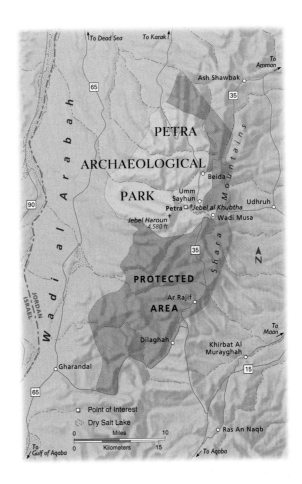

Its people—living in hundreds of villages in south and central Jordan, southern Syria, and the Negev desert—quickly learned the ways and crafts of Greece, Rome, and Egypt. At Petra their vision, skill, and doggedness made them champions at carving stone temples, tombs, amphitheaters, stairways, altars, obelisks. They had the patience to face a blank wall and chisel out an ornate facade, then a door frame, then a door, then a hollow, and finally a perfect chamber the size of a ballroom. The name Petra comes from the Greek word for "rock."

In A.D. 106, Roman Emperor Trajan annexed the rich region and incorporated it into the province of Arabia. Nabataean prosperity slowly declined when the provincial capital shifted northward and the caravan trade bypassed Petra. During the Byzantine period of the fourth, fifth, and sixth centuries Petra became a Christian site, but further decline followed, sped along periodically by devastating earthquakes. The subsequent arrival of Islam in the seventh century brought no

revival to this now remote backwater. In time the city was abandoned and the thread of Petra's history was lost.

But in the summer of 1812, Petra reappeared from dim memory. Johann Ludwig Burckhardt, a Swiss-German explorer and Arabist, was on his way to Cairo disguised as a Muslim trader from India—common practice among Europeans traveling in this part of the world where locals were wary of outsiders and fearful of spies. During his travels he had heard locals speak of a strange forgotten city hidden deep within the mountains. These stories sparked his interest, and he decided to investigate. Though Burckhardt spent only one day among the ruins, he was able to confirm that this was the Petra of ancient texts. Over the next 30 years, five European expeditions reached Petra, opening the door for scholarship, biblical studies, and intrepid travelers. Forgotten Petra reawoke.

I saw the results of that awakening from a spot 200 feet up the side of the mountain. At 8:20 a.m. exactly, the sun's rays hit the facade of the Treasury. A wave of gasps and clapping from tourist groups below met this daily spectacle of illumination. This was soon followed by the drone of a tour leader's voice and ceaseless chatter up and down the valley. Today as many as 4,000 tourists arrive daily. They come mostly in fume-belching buses and jostle their way along an approach route formed by a broad divided thoroughfare, pedestrians on one side, horses on the other. "Sunset Boulevard," the critics call it. Hardly an auspicious approach to such a glorious monument.

Despite what sometimes seems like rampant tourism, park development is, in fact, carefully monitored—much of it by Sa'ad Rawajfeh, director of planning for the Petra Regional Planning Council, who controls permits for all building inside the park. "Everything from water pipes to electric lines, from homes to hotels crosses my desk," he explains. On this day, like all others, petitioners line up outside his office door to plead their cases. They talk, argue, gesticulate, implore.

Escaping the petitioners, at least for an afternoon, Sa'ad took me south by jeep to his home village of Ar Rajif, where he had spent his childhood among siblings,

Appearing as if in a lightning bolt between cliffs, Al Khazneh, the Treasury, greets visitors as they approach the hidden city, which explorer Johann Burckhardt rediscovered in 1812.

Following pages: Bedouin watch from the Treasury as the latest tourist contingent arrives. Since 1991, annual visitation to Petra has leapt tenfold, to nearly half a million people.

goats, and the rhythm of the seasons. From the village we could see the park's vast broken landscape baking below, disappearing at the horizon in a white-hot haze. Petra National Park lies halfway between the Dead Sea and the Gulf of Aqaba. Its sandstone range, running north to south for the park's entire 35-mile length, but only 10 miles wide, stands out as the region's clearest landmark. Beyond to the west unfolds Wadi al Arabah, a vast basin of pale sand and rock that forms the lowest section of the park; at 700 feet below sea level it is one of the lowest spots on Earth.

"Bedouin still live there," noted Sa'ad, pointing to the most remote, forbidding spot in the desert landscape, "in caves, still living a virgin lifestyle. It is courageous, but very hard. As a boy, I went with friends to the wild places. We would make a fire under the stars. How free was the feeling, like being in heaven. Just one night in the desert—the shooting stars, the rising moon—is better than a week in hotel. Ah, the quiet.... But now life has become too complex."

We drove on to the park's southern limit, near the village of Dilaghah, where Sa'ad introduced me to a Bedouin family. Sixty-five-year-old Khalil greeted me with a rough, friendly handshake, led us into the shade of a long black tent, and asked us to recline on mattresses that lined the tent walls. The younger of his two wives soon arrived with strong, sweet tea flavored with mint leaves. She wore a full-length black dress embroidered at the hem, wrists, and chest with pendant patterns of bright gold thread. After tea she invited us to see her weaving—40-foot-long, 18-inch-wide strips of material made from shiny black goats' hair and decorated with bands of white sheep's wool. The strips are stitched together to make tents.

Then five boys came in and lined up at their father's side. Sa'ad translated for me as I asked, "How many children do you have?" "Sixteen," Khalil replied. "This is the youngest," he sighed, stroking the head of his three-year-old boy. Sixteen children! Sa'ad laughed. "I have eight! Ask anyone around here, it's all the same." Sure enough, the jeep driver had eleven. "Now we have more than 25,000 people living inside the borders of Petra park. The population is growing fast, so we have to be careful...try to limit the number of children."

Anxious to discover the undisturbed places in the park, I walked up into the jumbled mountains of Petra National Park. From afar they appeared accessible: the tallest were less than 5,000 feet, and the many wadis—here referring to dry streambeds—cut through them like pathways of approach. But once in the mountains, the configuration became a three-dimensional labyrinth of canyons, culs-de-sac, rock faces, and precipices. At higher elevations, a moment's deviation from the age-old paths led me to confusion. A mile away a line of goats, like black ants on a wall, traipsed

Though uninhabited by humans for centuries, Petra's desert still boasts a permanent population of arid-loving creatures, including this Blue Sinai lizard, here in its green phase.

single-file along a near-vertical face. Easy for them, but for me prudence prevailed.

Later, I sought out a guide who had been recommended to me: Salim Koplan, a serious man who knew Petra's hidden heart. He belonged to the Bedoul tribe. Until the early 1980s he and all his people lived in the region, as they had done for hundreds of years. Then, as part of a World Bank-sponsored project to preserve the archaeological monuments of ancient Petra, the Jordanian government moved them out en masse to a modern cement-and-cinder-block village called Umm Sayhun, two and a half miles away.

Salim spanned the modern and the traditional. He wore blue jeans, leather boots, and a down vest over a flannel shirt but was never without his red-and-white-checked *kaffiyeh* headdress and black oval *agal* to hold it in place. During our first meeting he reminisced about his early days: "At night, little lights in every cave, a white-robed man up in that one, goats and children on a ledge, women popping in and out of their cave homes. Yes, wonderful."

We agreed to see Petra's outback on foot and decided each day to go in a different direction. On our first day we headed west to Jebel Haroun—Aaron's

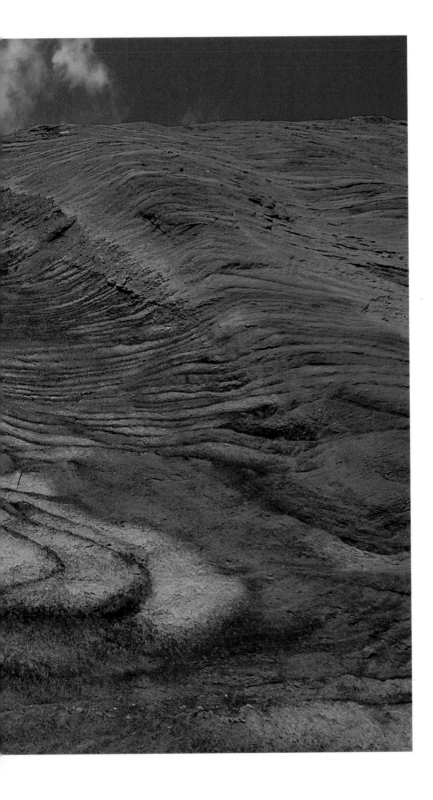

Fanciful designs in the sandstone cliffs of Petra have been carved not only by humans but by nature itself, which has been decorating the landscape for thousands of years. Water and wind reveal ancient strata and gouge natural caves in the towering faces of Petra's mountains.

Mountain—at 4,580 feet the highest in the range. Aaron, older brother of Moses, died here when Petra was the biblical land of Edom, and his tomb on the summit remains holy for Jews, Christians, and Muslims. We would make our own pilgrimage. Along the way, Salim showed me how to look under stones to find hidden creatures. Under one sandstone slab a yellow scorpion waited, pincers held high. It was waxy in appearance and more poisonous than the commoner black scorpion. It brandished its venomous tail for an instant before scuttling away.

"In old times, my mother protected us from scorpions," said Salim. "She took one yellow scorpion and one black one, roasted them in a fire, then ground them into powder. She put the powder on her breast while feeding the baby. I was the baby!" he exclaimed. "And when I drank the milk, I also took in this scorpion powder. So I am safe! I have been stung many times, on hand, arm, foot. Two years ago, sleeping outside in the desert, one scorpion was in my pants when I put them on in the morning.… Yow! But I am all right."

Astride a stone, I saw a brownish agama lizard, unremarkable except for its bold squat legs. But as it became aware of me, it slowly transformed itself, changing color through a range of greens finally to reach a startling azure blue that announced "stay away!" We went on in the midday glare, trudging up this mountain on well-worn paths as others had done for more than 33 centuries. Patches of utter silence were broken by a buzzing bee or my own footfall as I passed glittering yellow crocuses.

Just below the summit, near crumbled ruins of a Byzantine church, Salim indicated two foot-long glyphs incised into the stone—images of ibex. During years in the tomb-caves of Petra, Salim had only twice seen ibex. "They have all gone north, all gone away." He paused for a few moments, looked far into the distance, then talked of the region's largest predator, the striped hyena. It too had fared poorly, he explained, with probably fewer than 200 alive in Jordan. In the last two years, a car struck and killed one north of Wadi Musa; another was tracked and killed in its den. Leopards have not been seen for a generation, and gazelles have fled to remote Wadi al Arabah, some on into Israel to escape hunters.

At last we reached Aaron's tomb, a chest-high sarcophagus covered by a green shroud within a simple whitewashed, domed shrine. After a moment of silence we climbed several steep exterior stairs to the shrine's roof. Although dominated by the dome, the roof's flat areas functioned as perfect observation platforms. A gliding hawk far out over the wilderness led my eye to the limit of traditional Bedoul

Dressed for a wedding, a Bedouin woman wraps herself in traditions as durable as the city itself. Today, Bedouin are the cultural keepers of Petra.

A Bedouin bride tosses bread in preparation for her wedding. Her forebears greeted explorer Johann Burckhardt in 1812, when he recognized the ruined city as the legendary Petra, a city that had vanished from most maps by the seventh century.

land where, through binoculars, I saw black strips in the desert—Bedouin tents. The gray-green umbrellas of acacia trees afforded the only shade in the yellow desert. A dark smudge near the horizon marked irrigated Israeli fields.

The sight was a reminder that for millennia, gathering water has been perhaps the most critical human endeavor of all in this generally parched and forbidding region. For survival, the ancient Nabataeans created terraced hillsides to stem erosion, channels to carry water, dams to prevent flash floods, and cisterns to capture runoff from the mountains. The whole area is littered with remnants of these engineering achievements. On our descent, Salim showed me one excellent example of a catchment system, with the original underground cistern still intact. I walked down age-old steps into a 60-foot-long subterranean cavern. It was like a dark hangar. Fifteen graceful stone arches supported the roof above a pool of water—

water gathered in the same place and in the same manner as it was 2,000 years ago.

The next day we headed north to Beida, an area of Petra National Park renowned among the Bedoul for rapidly changing scenery and myriad canyons. Salim took me to a small, intact Nabataean dam, three feet tall and eight feet wide; behind it a ravine receded for 50 feet. The area had filled over the centuries with sand, stones, and debris. He mused: "Four Egyptian laborers…if I hire for six weeks…they can dig and clean…then we would have water for the Bedouin goats, lots of water. It is cold here, dark here, the sun won't take the water."

He guided me to an oleander-lined wadi and encouraged me to explore on my own while he prepared lunch. The streambed narrowed as it parted towering walls. The farther I went, the narrower it became until I could touch on both walls the tiger-striped rocks of deep red, maroon, and black, smoothed by age. The variety and sharp distinctions in color showed vividly the sedimentary history of the area's sandstone gorges. Though the desert was 85°F here, with almost no light, I quickly grew cold. Soon, ready for warmth and companionship, I returned to Salim.

He had a fire going, mint tea ready, and a lunch of flat bread warmed by the embers. The main course, sardines from a tin, tasted delicious. Salim had used the tin lid to slice open a lemon, then squeezed all of the juice onto the fish. For more tea, he instructed me to fetch firewood, but only from the *baloott* tree, a type of oak with a high rounded canopy of leaves. Salim proclaimed it "the best tree in Jordan, very strong. It is good for fires and burns a long time. Tea tastes best from a baloott fire outside." Tea was important to Salim. He keeps a steel cup, tea and sugar, a container of water, and a blackened kettle in a canvas satchel, always ready to go.

Our destination the third day was a wadi three hours by foot south from the center of Petra city. Along the way, Salim told me the Bedoul had a name for every place, mound, crest, cliff. As we crossed a plain, he announced that the Bedoul called it Al Aja—the Dusty Place. "In summer, a single goat crossing here, even a small wind—ah! dust, much dust. Dust rises up, fills the nose, the eyes…."

At a cluster of juniper trees, I learned from Salim that "long ago, before Ceylon tea, we Bedouin made juniper tea from these red, red berries. We call the tree *ar-ar*." More lore surrounded the waist-high ajram bush. "Bedouin soap," Salim called it. He took a handful of the flower heads, a bit of water, and rubbed his hands together energetically. "See." A pleasant-smelling froth emerged, and it did indeed clean his hands.

We pressed on to the wadi, ancient Petra's southern "suburb," a half-mile stretch of water and greenery in an elbow-bend of the oasis that once supported a town and caravansary. In the past, traders arriving from harsh weeks of desert exposure along the Red Sea route could drink their fill, wash the dust from their clothes and their camels, and prepare for a dignified entrance to the great city. As a vivid reminder of those lost days, seven camels chewed contentedly among the tall reeds of the oasis.

On our return, tromping through sand across a road still shored up with Nabataean yellow stone, Salim spotted three men on a ridge who were watching us. "These people," he said, "they are from the tribe of Saideen, from Wadi al Arabah." He greeted each of them warmly, many kisses on the cheeks, much repeated clasping of hands. The men, searching for lost goats, borrowed my binoculars and scanned canyons and mountainsides but to no avail. They all sat down in a circle to talk, and I wandered off.

Twenty minutes later they were in the same circular position, now with a smoky fire and tea at center. Salim looked at me over his shoulder and smiled. "Bedouin parliament!" He told me this is the way they meet to talk things over. Today the subjects are goats (lost), rain (none), and tribal relations. Some Bedoul land on the slopes of the Shara mountains has been planted without permission by men from Wadi Musa. This should not be. Also, one of the Saideen—in simple brown burnoose and broken plastic sandals—has no work and eight children to support, so Salim will seek permission for him to grow tobacco on this land to earn some money. He has also offered to hire this man to help rebuild a Nabataean dam. Salim believes he can find a cistern as well, long buried beneath his family's land within the park. Once he receives a permit to dig, the Saideen can clear the surface of the ground, perhaps to uncover ancient arches and stones. And perhaps Salim's dream of a small-scale revival of Nabataean hydrology will come true. "In ten years, or twenty years perhaps, then I die. But others can still use; if they clean every few years, maybe they can use forever!"

And so, Petra is neither timeless nor a dead city, but rather a unique monument of man and nature that requires a constant back-and-forth dialogue with the past and the present.

The last time I saw Salim he had stopped to visit with his mother, who lives most of her days far out in the desert on the trail between Petra and Jebel Haroun. From a distance I saw the silhouette of mother and son as she handed him something. It was a big bowl of cool water.

"Hydrology is the unseen beauty of Petra," says an engineer familiar with Nabataean ways of capturing rainwater using channels, dams, and rock-ribbed cisterns like this one.

Rarely visited by tourists, a nearby ruin known as Little Petra is a favorite relaxing spot for local Bedouin. On a fair spring day, with the poppies in full bloom, two men recline on the grass to discuss day-to-day issues over tea—a scene as timeless as the mysterious city that surrounds them.

Other National Parks of Note

Virachey National Park | Komodo National Park | Lushan National Park

Virachey National Park, Cambodia

In northeast Cambodia, pressed against the borders of Laos and Vietnam, lies heavily forested, sparsely populated Virachey National Park. One of Asia's largest protected areas at 1,283 square miles, Virachey contains little-explored forests that biologists believe shelter many species new to science. Small populations of the extremely rare Javan rhino and Indian tiger may be here as well. With rugged 3,000-foot mountains in the north and verdant valleys in the south, the park's isolation offers promise for habitat preservation; in Southeast Asia, where logging and destruction of rain forests have touched most areas, Virachey has a chance to hold the line.

Komodo National Park, Indonesia

At the heart of the Indonesian Archipelago, eight degrees south of the Equator, this Biosphere Reserve and UNESCO World Heritage site protects some 5,700 giant monitors known as Komodo dragons. Important to scientists who study evolution, these aggressive reptiles, the world's largest lizards, can reach 11 feet in length and live on small mammals, deer, boars, feral horses, even water buffalo. Komodo Island, the park's centerpiece, is surrounded by numerous volcanic isles where lontar palms dominate savanna plains. At higher elevations a broad flora exists with many endemic species. Neolithic graves, artifacts, and monoliths add a cultural dimension.

Lushan National Park, China

Lushan Mountain, rising abruptly from a watery plain, reaches nearly 5,000 feet to dominate northern Jiangxi Province. This World Heritage site, famous for cliffs, waterfalls, subtropical forests, bamboo groves, montane pools, and hundreds of floral species, affords magnificent views of the Yangtze River and huge Poyang Lake.

Tubbataha Reefs Marine National Park

Nanda Devi National Park

In ancient times, Lushan was a spiritual center for Buddhism, Taoism, and Confucianism—temples and pavilions still dot the mountainsides. In the past hundred years Lushan has become a retreat for missionaries and officials seeking relief from central China's torrid summers. Cool rains and morning mists keep the park's peaks and gorges lush throughout the year.

Tubbataha Reefs Marine National Park, Philippines

Tubbataha centers on the only two coral atolls in the Philippines, in the middle of the Sulu Sea, southeast of Palawan Island. This pristine environment of shoals and vertical reefs extends from just 6 feet above sea level to 330 below. As part of the Palawan Biosphere Reserve and a World Heritage site, Tubbataha supports a high diversity of fish (379 species recorded), sea turtles, and bird populations that include boobies and noddies. Though Tubbataha has no permanent population, its rich coral life draws some 1,500 visitors a year, mostly scuba divers.

Nanda Devi National Park, India

Among the most spectacular and unspoiled wilderness areas of the world, Nanda Devi National Park lies hidden within India's Garhwal Himalaya, just west of the Nepal border. At 25,648 feet, the Nanda Devi peak oversees a huge basin surrounded by steep cliffs and snowy mountains and divided by ridges and deep gorges with rushing rivers. This inner sanctuary of the Himalaya, a World Heritage site, has its own microclimate that makes the park wetter and lusher than comparable insular areas. Rare plants abound. Fourteen species of mammals, including the rare snow leopard, populate the mountain realm.

AUSTRALIA
AND THE SOUTH PACIFIC

Kakadu National Park

Joseph R. Yogerst

Thunder and lightning split the sky as I parked beside a billabong and started up a red-dirt track through a thicket of eucalyptus. The Big Wet, the northern Australia rainy season, wasn't due for a couple of months. But the air was already thick with moisture as I ambled toward a massive sandstone outcrop called Nourlangie Rock. Rarely do life and myth converge, but that seemed to be the case on this particular day, because I was soon face-to-face with Namarrgon, the Lightning Man of outback lore, peering down at me from his red-rock perch. We locked eyes, staring across a void that spanned several thousand years, one of those mystical moments that defies easy explanation. I knew the figure was nothing more than natural pigments on stone, yet there was something so lifelike in his rendering. And when lightning flashed again on the horizon, I felt that Namarrgon was speaking to me, spinning a story of romance, misfortune, and revenge.

Among the many ancient paintings covering Nourlangie, the Lightning Man depicts an Aboriginal creation hero, one of the mythic beings that inhabited the Earth prior to the birth of humans. He found his soul mate in a beautiful goddess named Barrkinj, and the two of them fell hopelessly in love. But then tragedy struck. An evil spirit abducted her, and ever since Namarrgon has wandered the Earth searching for his lost love. He vents his anger with electrical fury, scorching the land with his lightning bolts in an endless quest to flush the evil spirit from his hiding place. Which is one way of explaining why this northern extreme of Australia's Northern Territory spawns more lightning than about any other spot on the planet.

Rendered in ocher, black, white, and other outback hues, images of Aboriginal women march across Nourlangie Rock, one of 7,000 rock-art sites within the park.

Preceding pages: Early morning steam rises from Jim Jim Creek in the vast tropical floodplain that forms the heart of Kakadu National Park.

Much of Namarrgon's realm is protected within the confines of Kakadu National Park, Australia's largest and wildest conservation area. Established in 1979 and gradually enlarged over the years, Kakadu sprawls across an area as big as New Jersey (7,628 square miles). The name derives from an Aboriginal language called Gagudju, spoken in the region until the early 20th century. The modern-day descendants of the Gagudju continue to call Kakadu home, partners with the federal government in managing the huge park.

Kakadu embraces almost the entire watershed of the South Alligator River, covering six distinct ecological zones: tidal flats, floodplains, savanna woodlands, monsoon rain forests, sandstone escarpments, and granite ranges. Each contains unique inhabitants and unusual landscapes. Which means that Kakadu's biodiversity is also astounding: 1,600 plant species, nearly 300 bird types, and 64 kinds of mammal. No other Australian park can boast such diversity. "There are so many things that make this place special," says park manager Manfred Haala, Kakadu's top civil servant. "It's a living cultural landscape with a rich tapestry of rock art. It has wetlands of international importance. It has outstanding examples of ongoing ecological processes, biological evolution, and man's interaction with the environment."

But Kakadu's rugged terrain, in league with the region's dramatic weather, makes it a challenge for even the most intrepid of visitors. During the December-to-April monsoon season much of the park is virtually inaccessible. And even during the arid months between May and September, relying on a four-wheel-drive vehicle—and a sturdy pair of hiking boots—is the most practical way to explore the Kakadu backcountry. The park attracts about a quarter million visitors each year, but most don't stray very far from the paved roads. Vast tracts here remain pristine wilderness, barely touched by human hands.

Like nearly everyone who visits Kakadu, my gateway was Darwin, the Northern Territory's rough-and-tumble capital. Rounding a corner late at night, I came upon two young women in short black dresses blocking the middle of the road. They were going round and round, holding tight to one another's arms, and at first I thought they were dancing—until they started to throw punches. One of the combatants shoved the other over the hood of a car and was ready to strike with a spiked heel when Darwin's finest arrived. It was a wake-up call, a reminder that the Top End has never been properly "civilized" and that things were bound to get even wilder in Kakadu.

The following morning I headed into the outback in a rented Land Cruiser, traveling south and then east across the coastal plains. It was a wonderful morning—blue sky with billowy white clouds in the distance. And a marvelous road too, as smooth as silk with wide curves and long straightaways. By the time I reached the Adelaide River, I was well into the outback wilderness that shelters the western flank of Kakadu, driving through broad spear-grass plains threaded by rivers overhung by pandanus. On the high ground, stands of eucalyptus waved gracefully in the wind.

Nobody knows the Adelaide like Peter McKenna, a rotund, robust, and deeply tanned outfitter who makes a living taking fishermen and sightseers up and down the river. "You wanna keep that arm, don't hang it over the side," he warned in his Aussie twang as we pulled away from the dock in his flat-bottom tour boat and headed upriver for an hour-long cruise. A warning was hardly necessary. I'd already

Australia's largest and most diverse national park, Kakadu embraces six distinct ecosystems spread across a vast expanse of the Northern Territory.

Following pages: Tidal flats along the Kakadu coast are a gathering place for millions of migratory waterbirds, like these little corellas. The estuaries also provide a rich breeding ground for fish, including the fierce barramundi.

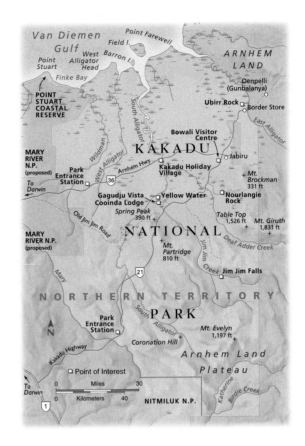

read about saltwater crocodiles in a safety brochure distributed by the Kakadu park authorities. The pamphlet implores visitors not to swim in local billabongs (the Aussie term for oxbow lakes) and rivers. "Tragic death and injury have occurred in the park due to crocodile attacks," it states rather bluntly.

The amphibious reptiles are naturally aggressive, especially when protecting their nests. And they are definitely man-eaters, Pete reassured me, launching into a yarn about a local fisherman who had the misfortune to fall asleep on a boat ramp after one too many beers. "Next morning the police found part of his body on shore and the rest inside the belly of a 16-foot croc," Peter related. As if that weren't enough to make me respect—and fear—the creatures, Peter baited a fishing line with pork and dangled it over the gunwale. Within seconds a dark reptilian form was making a beeline toward our boat. Peter raised the bait until it was a good ten feet above the surface. But that didn't faze the croc; it jumped right out of the water, its jaws slamming around the meat like a steel trap.

Safely back in my car on dry land, I soon passed through the park entrance

Using methods pioneered by his ancestors thousands of years ago, an Aboriginal boy hoists his fishing spear above an Arnhem Land creek. Recreational fishing—by ancient or modern methods—is still allowed in Kakadu's myriad waterways.

and began the long drive across the floodplains that dominate the heart of Kakadu. This vast sea of grass and water bears more than a passing resemblance to Florida's Everglades—a maze of wetlands and waterways where hundreds of rivers, swamps, and billabongs meander and mingle with each new rainy season. The rivers are heavily tidal, with saltwater reaching as far as 50 miles inland and the water level rising and falling dramatically in just several hours. It's a paradise for migratory waterbirds, with as many as two and a half million at any one time using Kakadu as a way station on their long journeys to and from Asia.

Ridges and rises between the watercourses shelter lush savanna woodlands, which support a greater variety of flora and fauna than any other section of the park. The dominant plant species is the paperbark or eucalyptus tree, which makes for cool shade during bush walks. But don't expect to see koalas; the forests of Kakadu are far beyond their normal range. During the rainy season, the area becomes a vast swamp virtually impossible to cross in anything other than a boat. But this was the dry season and the great wetlands were hot and parched, smaller rivers running at a trickle, many of the billabongs dry.

As I piloted my Land Cruiser down the Arnhem Highway, I watched the vehicle's air temperature gauge soar to nearly 90°F. But that didn't dissuade me from stopping here and there, setting off into the bush on foot. The nature trail at an area called Mamukala proved especially rewarding. A lookout point beside the trail gave me a close-up view of thousands of magpie geese feasting on the plains. When something startled them into taking flight, the sky suddenly went dark with their black-and-white profiles.

Catching a whiff of smoke in the air, I cranked my head around to the east. On the horizon, blazing on the far side of Kakadu, was a bushfire—great billows of smoke roiling up from the plains, possibly ignited by my old friend Namarrgon but more likely set by park rangers. For thousands of years, local Aborigines have used dry-season fires to purge the land of brush so that new grass can more easily take root and prosper when the rainy season arrives. The new grass, called green pick, attracts a bounty of game animals—wallabies, possums, and goanna lizards. Burning also helps stimulate the natural harvest of yams, the main staple of the native diet, and reduces the risk of wildfires burning out of control. When Kakadu became a national park, authorities decided to carry on the Aboriginal tradition as a means of preserving the unique balance between natural and man-made forces that has characterized the region for millennia.

A pack of dingoes, their golden eyes reflected in my headlights, scampered across the road as I coasted into Jabiru, a ragtag collection of workers' homes and a big hotel, all associated with the park headquarters here. Over the next week, I would range out from Jabiru on various forays into Kakadu's backcountry. But I also figured the small outback town was a good place to get a handle on the political forces that help shape the park, the unusual and sometimes stormy partnership between the federal government, local Aboriginal clans, and private enterprise.

Today, Kakadu's land is owned and managed jointly by local Aboriginal groups like the Gagudju and Jabiluka and by the Australian National Parks and Wildlife Service; native members represent a majority of Kakadu's management board. Seventy percent of the operational budget comes from the federal coffers in Canberra, the bulk from visitor entrance fees. But much of the infrastructure development—hotels, restaurants, guide services—is funded by the Aboriginal communities, paid for with royalties derived from uranium mines on native land claims inside the park.

Saltwater crocodiles are well entrenched at the top of the Kakadu food chain, feeding regularly on barramundi, wallabies, and other large prey. Hunted for hides and sport, the world's largest reptiles were nearly exterminated in the decades following World War II, but have made a spectacular recovery within the park since hunting was banned in 1971.

An outback moon hovers above Jim Jim Creek, fed by two spectacular waterfalls that tumble down from the red-rock Stone Country.

"The biggest challenge of managing a park like Kakadu is trying to deal with all the competing interests that are part of this place," administrator Manfred Haala explained to me. "Things like tourism versus culture versus the natural environment. This happens on all the different issues, whether it's weeds, fire, or interpretation planning. It doesn't matter. The aim, of course, is balancing all these interests." Which isn't always easy. One of the managers of the Gagudju Crocodile Hotel—a joint venture between native investors and an international hospitality firm—admitted that the arrangement was less than fluid. "They must be consulted every time we want to do something," he admitted, referring to the Aboriginal council. "For example, if we want to build a tennis court, the council must approve it."

Taking off from the Jabiru airstrip the next morning, I got a bird's-eye view of the giant Ranger Mine, a massive orange scar dug into the land to extract uranium and one of the trade-offs the Australian park service was willing to make in order to protect the rest of Kakadu from development and exploitation. At the controls of the small sightseeing plane I had hired was a pilot who looked barely old enough to graduate from high school, let alone fly. But with a deft touch he guided us into a tight turn and we headed south, leaving the mine behind.

Almost at once the majesty of Kakadu spread out before us: the immense plains, the great eucalyptus forests, the swirling blue rivers and oxbow lakes. I was so busy scanning the scenery below I didn't notice a red-rock wall rearing up before us—the first outrider of the Arnhem Land Plateau.

Locals call this part of the park the Stone Country, a massive sandstone mantle that stands firm against the ravages of wind, rain, and time, a striking tribute to the geologic forces that have shaped Australia. The escarpments—monumental swirls of stone scarred with fissures and crevices that look as if they had been hacked by some giant ax—are mostly void of vegetation. But amid all this rock I could pick out tiny islands of life, lush monsoon forest thriving in the deeper canyons and gorges, isolated Gardens of Eden that took root around permanent water holes and creeks.

"Few people get up this way," the pilot declared as we banked sharply and winged our way up another creek. Dead ahead, a thin stream of water plunged down the escarpment—650-foot-high Jim Jim Falls—one of the park's most inspiring sights and one of its most difficult to reach. The only way to view the cascade at ground level is to drive 40 miles along one of the roughest, most bone-rattling tracks in Australia. Yet a few intrepid souls had managed to make the trek. I could see them far below, lounging in the deep blue plunge pool at the base of Jim Jim, their tents nestled in the nearby woods.

We left the escarpment behind and followed the sinuous path of the South Alligator River toward the coast. The name is a relic from early white settlers who mistook the crocodiles for their North American cousins. Unlike some of the other Kakadu rivers that peter out in dense swamps, the South Alligator flows majestically into the Van Diemen Gulf, slowly but surely pressing its delta farther into the sea, enriching offshore waters for a hundred miles in either direction.

Although Indonesian fishermen had known this coast for centuries, trading and often mating with local Aborigines, the shore was officially "discovered" in 1623 by Dutch navigator Willem Van Coolsteerdt, sailing south from Java in an effort to find a passage between Australia and New Guinea. It was a harsh environment, rife with saltwater crocodiles, malarial swamps, and hostile tribes, and the Dutch made no effort to colonize or even barter with the locals. The British didn't either, even after they had wrested Terra Australis from the Dutch. In fact, the Top End wasn't settled by outsiders until the mid-19th century. Even then, the Kakadu coast

Wallaroos relax in a savanna woodland clearing. A testament to its isolation and mankind's determination to preserve it, Kakadu ranks as the only major Australian ecosystem that has recorded no extinction of plants or animals over the last 200 years.

remained immune to permanent settlement, with a scattering of nomadic Aborigines and white buffalo hunters.

Centuries of human disinterest have left Kakadu's coastal belt in its original condition. Unsullied by industrial pollution, agricultural runoff, and human waste, the area harbors mangrove swamps and associate life-forms, including more than 350 species of plants. The brackish rivers are also a nursery for many different types of fish, including the tasty and sometimes dangerously aggressive *barramundi* (sea bass). Not far offshore is Field Island—the park's northern extreme—a nesting site for several species of sea turtles and home to the extremely rare Australian dugong.

I got a closer look at the South Alligator River at a place called Yellow Water, a chain of billabongs south of Jabiru. In the rainy season, the area is one huge swamp. But during the dry months, Yellow Water transforms into a local version of an African water hole, a place where wild creatures of every shape and size come to drink. It's considered one of the best places in the entire park to view wildlife.

Yellow Water offers several short hiking trails, including an elevated path that leads out over the swamps. But the best way to explore the billabongs is a tour on a flat-bottom boat. My skipper was Glenn Dickson, a young Aussie with the dark tan and muscular frame of a rugby player. He certainly knew his wildlife. And like many of the locals I met during my trip to Kakadu, he liked to "take the mickey" out of unsuspecting visitors.

After watching a couple of tourists battle mosquitoes on the dock, Glenn broke into a wide smile. "There's not much of a problem with malaria in Kakadu," he announced over the microphone. "Just a few isolated cases. A more serious problem here is Ross River virus, which is also transmitted by mossies. It can last a few years, put you in the hospital." That sent the tourists into an even greater frenzy of bug spraying and swatting.

With the obligatory outback prank behind us, we settled into cruising down one billabong and then up another, a journey that took us past grasslands and thick wads of paperbark. All around was unfettered nature, animals that hardly seemed to notice our presence: thousands of migratory waterbirds—herons, egrets, jacanas, and geese—and shaggy wild horses grazing a spear-grass meadow. And a host of creepy crawlies: goanna lizards slithering through the mud; snakes coiled around the branches of riverside trees; and dozens upon dozens of crocodiles sleeping on the banks, sneaking through the shallows, and fighting over the dwindling patches of water—more crocodiles than I had ever seen in the wild in a single day.

"During the wet season the crocs migrate downstream to build their nests and hatch their eggs," Glenn explained. "They don't come back up to Yellow Water and other inland billabongs until the water level gets lower and the banks start to reappear." I asked Glenn if the giant reptiles are still considered endangered. He shook his head emphatically. "Not in these parts. It's estimated there are up to 80,000 crocodiles in the Northern Territory alone, and there's even some talk of culling them again in limited numbers."

On the drive back from Yellow Water, I popped in to see the Lightning Man at Nourlangie Rock and the dozens of other ancient paintings that share his red-rock home. Some 7,000 rock paintings have been discovered throughout Kakadu—a record of Aboriginal life and thought during the past 20,000 years. The images depict various gods and demons, and mythological and Dreamtime stories, but they also tell us how the ancient people of Kakadu lived, what sort of animals they hunted, the kinds of plants they ate, what they wore as clothing and jewelry, and what contacts they had with people from other regions. Yams, for example, seem to have been an important source of food in centuries past, and Aborigines apparently once hunted animals like the Tasmanian tiger and long-beaked echidna, both now extinct. One painting even offered a pictorial parable about a brother and sister who were banished from their tribe for committing incest. There were also pictures of a European sailing ship and a flintlock pistol thought to have been painted around 400 years ago, after Dutch navigators first visited the Kakadu coast.

Given their style, many of the images are believed to be between 2,000 and 6,000 years old, and carbon dating of human artifacts found nearby proves that people have lived at Nourlangie for more than 20,000 years. Most of the paintings are originals, but it's known that a local Aboriginal artist named Barramundi Charlie, who lived here in the 1960s, repainted many of the ancient masterpieces that had faded over the years—a common Aboriginal practice.

Many of Kakadu's modern-day artists reside in a sleepy little village called Oenpelli on the eastern fringe of the park. As is so often true of Kakadu's gems, Oenpelli demands careful planning and a large dose of determination to reach.

Heeding advice printed on the park map, I ducked into the Bowali Visitor Center in Jabiru before setting off. A burly ranger with tree-stump legs and a red beard confirmed my worst fears: "The East Alligator River's pretty high, mate. Doubt you can get across... unless you've got four-wheel drive." It just so happened that I did, although I had never actually used it to ford deep water. But the ranger gave me precise instructions on how to cross the river and sent me on my way, probably figuring I'd be back in a couple of hours—after I'd taken one look at the Alligator. "One last piece of advice," he grinned. "If you get stuck, don't jump out and try to make it back to the bank. If the current doesn't kill ya, the crocs'll get ya for sure."

In no hurry to test my vehicle's amphibious skills, I took my time driving up to the East Alligator, a meandering route through some of the finest scenery Kakadu has to offer—spear-grass meadows, thick eucalyptus forests punctuated by red-rock

Life burgeons along an outback creek near Jabiru. A long monsoon season, between December and April, transforms the Kakadu backcountry into a vibrant coat of many colors.

Following pages: Kakadu's version of Ayers Rock, a red-rock monolith called Nourlangie, rises high above the floodplains. For more than 20,000 years, Aboriginal people have sought refuge—and rendered artistic magic—in Nourlangie's crevices and caverns.

outcroppings, and no shortage of wildlife. A black snake curled up in the middle of the road, a wallaroo bounded beside a billabong, a flock of pink-and-white cockatoos took flight. With the windows down, I could smell the sweet scent of the eucalyptus groves all around. I lingered at Ubirr Rock long enough to scale the great 820-foot monolith and admire its rock-art galleries.

It was enough to lull me into a false sense of security. Then I saw the river. A white-water torrent pouring down from the Arnhem highlands, it covered the roadway for more than a hundred yards. At first I thought about turning around and packing it in right then. But I wasn't up to facing that ranger again, admitting outright defeat. This was do or die. Oenpelli or bust. I popped the Land Cruiser into four-wheel drive and slipped into the water, taking it slow and steady, making sure I didn't veer too far to the left or right, lest I plunge off the stone causeway into even deeper water. Waves beat against the side of the truck and water started seeping beneath the driver's side door. It took me about five minutes to reach the other bank, soaked in sweat and river water and tremendously relieved that the fording had gone so well.

Another half hour up the track along a road flanked by billabongs and orange cliffs and I was in Oenpelli. A typical Aboriginal township, it was no more than a cluster of small wooden houses with tin roofs whose red-dirt yards sprouted tufts of grass. Dominating the town was the long, cinder-block presence of the Injalak Arts and Crafts Center, a gathering place for native talent from all around Arnhem Land. "In the late 1980s, Aboriginal artists from this area got together and said they wanted their own place to paint, show, and sell their own art," artist Leslie Nawirridj explained to me as he fashioned blades of grass into a makeshift paintbrush. "Without Injalak a lot of us would be unemployed."

Injalak's main art form is painting—traditional designs rendered on bark or cotton paper imported from France. But basket weaving, jewelry making, wood carving, and screen printing are also done. Artwork produced here has been shown at galleries throughout the world, in such diverse places as Sydney, New York, and Munich, and the center has provided more than 40 paintings for a new Aboriginal art museum in the United States.

About half a dozen artists are "in residence" at any given time, painting beneath a veranda that runs along either side of the administration building, carving, or weaving baskets beneath the trees in the garden. Most of the paintings are rendered in the classic Aboriginal "X-ray" style that depicts the inner skeleton and organs of the various human and animal subjects. Ocher is the dominant color, but red, yellow, white, and black are also prevalent. Leslie and the other artists mix the colors on the concrete floor by grinding natural clays, minerals, or charcoal and then mixing them with water. The paint is applied with brushes made from human hair,

Watched by his son Peter, Aboriginal artist Lofty Habardayal creates a bark painting. Kakadu's artistic heritage endures in the Aboriginal settlements in and around the park.

Following pages: Pandanus fringe the park's Mamukala wetlands. The trees feed many animal species, as well as Aborigines, who use stingray tails to gouge out the nuts.

feathers, roots, grass, and strips of bark—or else is blown from the artist's mouth. "We only use real paintbrushes for thick stuff," Leslie explained. "When I do fine lines and crosshatching, I always use grass."

It was a great solace for me to discover that the cultural forces responsible for Namarrgon and the other Nourlangie masterpieces are still alive and well in Kakadu. Like their ancient ancestors, the artists of Injalak express what they see in the landscape—the furious lightning that ushers in the rainy season, the magpie geese and barramundi that prowl the wetlands, and the various Dreamtime stories that explain the origin of our species—the ever changing drama that makes Kakadu one of the world's great national parks.

Other National Parks of Note

Fiordland National Park   Great Barrier Reef Marine Park   Mount Cook National Park

Fiordland National Park, New Zealand

On the shore of the Tasman Sea lies New Zealand's largest preserve, 4,850 square miles of pristine wilderness tucked in the southwest corner of South Island. Ice Age glaciers carved deep valleys along the coast, creating the park's fjords and lakes. Snowcapped peaks rise beside majestic bodies of water like Milford Sound and Lake Te Anau. The area's heavy rainfall (as much as 300 inches per year) feeds wild rivers and some of the world's highest waterfalls. Fiordland's lush evergreen forest supports a profusion of indigenous birdlife, including the kiwi, kakapo, and kea parrot.

Great Barrier Reef Marine Park, Australia

As the name suggests, Great Barrier Reef Marine Park safeguards the world's largest accumulation of coral, a living necklace that stretches 1,250 miles down the Queensland coast. The park encompasses all or parts of 11 major islands, including such popular resorts as Heron, Dunk, Brampton, and the Whitsundays. Scuba divers flock to the turquoise waters, but the reef can also be explored by sail, glass-bottom boat, and even submarine.

In addition to 400 coral species, the reef supports more than 240 bird species and diverse tropical flora.

Mount Cook National Park, New Zealand

Mount Cook National Park—one of the Earth's most impressive collections of rock, ice, and snow—crowns the middle of the South Island. The reserve takes its name from New Zealand's highest summit (12,349-foot Mount Cook) and preserves 20 other peaks over 10,000 feet. A third of the park's 270 square miles is covered in permanent snow and ice, including the spectacular Fox and Tasman Glaciers. Needless to say, mountain climbing and snow skiing are the main attractions, with many of the more challenging areas accessible only by helicopter or bush plane.

Nitmiluk National Park

Southwest National Park

Uluru National Park

Nitmiluk National Park, Australia

Along the banks of the Katherine River—another remarkable expanse of the Aussie outback—lies Nitmiluk National Park. The heart of the park is a sequence of 13 red-rock canyons collectively known as Katherine Gorge. A paradise for water sports enthusiasts, the gorge is accessible by canoe, kayak, or tour boat. Another way to traverse Nitmiluk is a five-day hiking trail dotted by wilderness campsites.

Southwest National Park, Australia

Tasmania's wild and rugged Southwest National Park is one of the most remote corners of the South Pacific. Unlike other parts of the island, this massive expanse of temperate rain forest was spared the chainsaw after years of conflict between timber companies and environmentalists. Sweeping back from the jagged coast, the forest is home to such massive trees as the swamp gum and Huon pine, some of them thousands of years old. Moss,

lichen, and ferns complete the sylvan mosaic. Very few roads penetrate the region, and the park is best explored by foot, boat, or bush plane.

Uluru National Park, Australia

Australia's relentless desert comes into full bloom at Uluru National Park, which protects both Ayers Rock and a cluster of red-rock monoliths called the Olgas. You can explore both of these natural landmarks on foot via a system of trails that wind through oasis canyons and past caves garnished with ancient rock art. This part of the desert is rife with Dreamtime lore and harbors a number of sacred Aboriginal sites. Founded in 1958, the park is managed by a local native clan in cooperation with the federal park service.

NOTES ON THE CONTRIBUTORS

PATRICK BOOZ was born in Beirut, Lebanon, and grew up in South and Southeast Asia. A graduate of the University of Wisconsin, where he studied Asian history and Chinese and Indonesian languages, he has spent half his life in Asia—including ten years in China and Hong Kong. Though specializing in China and Tibet, he retains a keen interest in the Middle East and Indonesia, where he resided for three years. He presently lives in Sweden with his wife, Ingrid, a photographer, and their two small children.

DOUGLAS BENNETT LEE, a freelance writer, filmmaker, and photographer, grew up in Manila, Tokyo, Kuwait, and London. Since visiting Botswana's Okavango Delta on assignment for NATIONAL GEOGRAPHIC magazine in 1988, he has lived intermittently in South Africa and its neighboring countries. A 14-year career as a GEOGRAPHIC staff writer also took him on extended explorations of Alaska and the Canadian Arctic, Louisiana's Gulf Coast, and the wilds of northern Japan. Recent freelance work in Africa includes writing and producing *Snakes: Africa's Deadly Dozen,* a film for National Geographic Television. He currently resides on Maryland's Eastern Shore.

California-based JOSEPH R. YOGERST has written for numerous international publications, including the *Washington Post, Los Angeles Times,* and *Condé Nast Traveler.* He is a four-time winner of the Society of American Travel Writers' Lowell Thomas Award. His last National Geographic book, *Long Road South: The Pan American Highway,* was chosen by SATW as one of the top two travel books of 1999. He is currently writing an action-adventure film set in the South Pacific for Sony Pictures.

ACKNOWLEDGMENTS

The Book Division and the writers and photographers of this book would like to thank the following people: Luis Alfaro, Ada Castillo, Dr. Stephanie Freitag, Kit Herring, Ingemar Johnsson, William Mabasa, Elizabeth Mholongo, Helen Mmethi, Charles Munn, Patricia Ortiz, Peter Scott, Marissa Silvera, and Josefina Tamaki. In addition, we thank Rebecca Lescaze and Carolinda E. Averitt for their careful reading of the final manuscript.

ADDITIONAL READING

T. Press, D. Lea, A. Wegg, and A. Graham (eds), *Kakadu: Natural and Cultural Heritage and Management;* Bob Scholes (text) and Nigel J. Dennis (photography), *The Kruger National Park: Wonders of an African Eden;* Kim MacQuarrie, *Manu: Amazon Eden of Peru;* D. Canestrier, N. Loury, J-P Potron, and R. Settimo, *l'ABCdaire du Mercantour;* Rosalyn Maqsood, *Petra: A Traveller's Guide;* Noel Grove, "Alaska's Sky High Wilderness," NATIONAL GEOGRAPHIC, May 1994; *Last Wild Places,* National Geographic Society. The reader may consult the *National Geographic Index* for other related articles and books.

PHOTO CREDITS

Cover, Manoj Shah/stone; back cover, up left, Fred Hirschmann; up right, Vincent J. Musi; low left, Annie Griffiths Belt; low right, Theo Allofs; 1, Theo Allofs; 2-3, Art Wolfe/stone; 7, Tom Bol/Tom Bol Photography; 10-11, Kevin Schafer; 13, Kevin Schafer; 16-17, André Bärtschi; 18-19, André Bärtschi; 21, André Bärtschi; 22-23, Art Wolfe/Art Wolfe, Inc.; 24, Patricio Robles Gil; 25 upper, André Bärtschi; 25 lower, André Bärtschi; 27, André Bärtschi; 28-29, Art Wolfe/Art Wolfe, Inc.; 30, André Bärtschi; 32-33, Kevin Schafer; 35, André Bärtschi; 36, André Bärtschi; 38-39, André Bärtschi; 40 left, Kevin Schafer/Peter Arnold, Inc.; 40 center, Aldo Brando/Peter Arnold, Inc.; 40 right, Chad Ehlers/stone; 41 left, Kevin Schafer/Peter Arnold, Inc.; 41 center, Simeone Huber/stone; 41 right, Art Wolfe/stone; 42-43, Joshua Foreman; 45, Theo Allofs; 48-49, Rich Reid/Colors of Nature; 50, Fred Hirschmann; 53, Art Wolfe/Art Wolfe, Inc.; 54, Ken Graham/Ken Graham Agency; 56-57, Rich Reid/Colors of Nature; 58-59, Fred Hirschmann; 60-61, George Mobley/NGP; 62, Howie Garber/Ken Graham Agency; 64, Tom Bean/stone; 65, Rich Reid/Colors of Nature; 67, George Mobley/NGP; 68-69, Ray Scott; 70-71, Art Wolfe/Art Wolfe, Inc.; 72 left, Jonathan Tourtellot/NGS Image Collection; 72 center, Phil Schermeister/stone; 72 right, Johan Elzenga/stone; 73 left, Chris Johns/NGP; 73 center, Brian Skerry/NGS Image Collection; 73 right, Norbert Rosing/NGS Image Collection; 74-103, Vincent J. Musi; 104 left, Jan-Peter Lahall/Peter Arnold, Inc.; 104 center, Tim Pickering; 104 right, Fred Bruemmer/Peter Arnold, Inc.; 105 left, Jeffrey Aaronson; 105 right, James P. Blair/NGS Image Collection; 106-107, Sean Lindsay/CCAfrica; 109, Marilyn Mofford Gibbons; 112-113, Chris Johns/NGP; 114, Marilyn Mofford Gibbons; 115, Marilyn Mofford Gibbons; 116-117, Chris Johns/NGP; 118, Chris Johns/NGP; 119, Theo Allofs; 120-121, Jannie Naude/CCAfrica; 123, Chris Johns/NGP; 124, Jannie Naude/CCAfrica; 126-127, Jannie Naude/CCAfrica; 129, Kevin Schafer; 130-131, Chris Johns/NGP; 133, Chris Johns/NGP; 134, Sean Lindsay/CCAfrica; 135, Richard Brugman/CCAfrica; 136-137, Chris Johns/NGP; 139, Marilyn Mofford Gibbons; 140-141, Maurice Hornocker/NGS Image Collection; 142 left, Jason Lauré; 142 center, Kenneth Love/NGS Image Collection; 142 right, Guido A. Rossi/Image Bank; 143 left, Michael K. Nichols/NGP; 143 center, Janis Carter; 143 right, Kazuyoshi Nomachi; 144-167, Annie Griffiths Belt; 168 left, Dieter & Mary Plage; 168 center, Albert Visage/Peter Arnold, Inc.; 168 right, Zi Qing Li/Image Bank; 169 left, Lynn Funkhouser/Peter Arnold, Inc.; 169 right, John P. Kelly/Image Bank; 170-171, Theo Allofs; 173, Glen Allison/stone; 176-177, Richard Woldendorp; 178, Penny Tweedie/stone; 180-181, Daniel J. Cox/Natural Exposures; 182, Theo Allofs; 184, Gerry Ellis/ENP Images; 187, R. Ian Lloyd; 188-189, Matthias Breiter/Oxford Scientific Films; 191, Ira Block; 192-193, Theo Allofs; 194 left, Christopher Arnesen/stone; 194 center, J.P. Ferrero/Auscape/Peter Arnold Inc; 194 right, Paul Chesley/stone; 195 left, Index Stock Imagery; 195 center, Melinda Berge; 195 right, Paul Chesley/stone

Index

Composition for this book by the National Geographic Society Book Division. Printed and bound by R.R. Donnelley & Sons, Willard, Ohio. Color separations by Digital Color Image, Pennsauken, NJ. Dust jacket printed by Miken Inc.

ENDURING TREASURES
National Parks of the World

Published by the National Geographic Society

John M. Fahey, Jr. *President and Chief Executive Officer*

Gilbert M. Grosvenor *Chairman of the Board*

Nina D. Hoffman *Senior Vice President*

Prepared by the Book Division

William R. Gray *Vice President and Director*

Charles Kogod *Assistant Director*

Barbara A. Payne *Editorial Director and Managing Editor*

Staff for this Book

K. M. Kostyal *Project Editor*

Richard Busch *Text Editor*

Marilyn Mofford Gibbons *Illustrations Editor*

Cinda Rose *Art Director*

Joyce M. Caldwell *Researcher*

Carl Mehler *Director of Maps*

Joseph F. Ochlak *Map Researcher*

Matt Chwastyk *Map Production*
Mapping Specialists
Jerome N. Cookson
Gregory Ugiansky

Tibor G. Tóth *Map Relief*

R. Gary Colbert *Production Director*

Lewis R. Bassford *Production Project Manager*

Richard S. Wain *Production Manager*

Janet A. Dustin *Illustrations Assistant*

Peggy J. Candore *Assistant to the Director*

Dale-Marie Herring *Staff Assistant*

Mark A. Wentling *Indexer*

Manufacturing and Quality Management

George V. White *Director*

John T. Dunn *Associate Director*

Vincent P. Ryan *Manager*

Phillip L. Schlosser *Financial Analyst*

Library of Congress Cataloging-in-Publication Data

Enduring treasures : national parks of the world.
    p. cm.
    ISBN 0-7922-7864-X—ISBN 0-7922-7865-8
    1. National parks and reserves. I. National Geographic Society (U.S.)

SB481.E53 2000
333.78'316—dc1   00-041841

The world's largest nonprofit scientific and educational organization, the National Geographic Society was founded in 1888 "for the increase and diffusion of geographic knowledge." Since then it has supported scientific exploration and spread information to its more than nine million members worldwide.

The National Geographic Society educates and inspires millions every day through magazines, books, television programs, videos, maps and atlases, research grants, the National Geography Bee, teacher workshops, and innovative classroom materials.

The Society is supported through membership dues and income from the sale of its educational products. Members receive NATIONAL GEOGRAPHIC magazine—the Society's official journal—discounts on Society products, and other benefits.

For more information about the National Geographic Society and its educational programs and publications, please call 1-800-NGS-LINE (647-5463), or write to the following address:

National Geographic Society
1145 17th Street N.W.
Washington, D.C. 20036-4688
U.S.A.

Visit the Society's Web site at
www.nationalgeographic.com
.